a
Practitioner's Guide
to
reflection
in Service-Learning:

STUDENT VOICES
& REFLECTIONS

Janet Eyler • *Dwight E Giles Jr* • *Angela Schmiede*

VANDERBILT UNIVERSITY • NASHVILLE, TN • 1996

A Technical Assistance Project funded by The Corporation for National Service

This material is based upon work supported by the Corporation for National Service under Cooperative Agreement No. CA94-08.

Any opinions, findings, and conclusions or recommendations expressed in this material are those of the authors and do not necessarily reflect the views of the Corporation for National Service.

GRAPHIC DESIGN, PRODUCTION AND EDITING BY DEBORAH AXT

THANK YOU

We are grateful first of all to the 67 students from eight colleges and universities who generously shared their time, insights, and service experiences with us. It is *their* thoughts about service and reflection, and *their* recollections of the activities and assignments that were most meaningful to them, that form the subject matter of this guide.

We also wish to thank the service-learning professionals who worked with us to arrange student interviews on their campuses:

◆ Dr. Ed Zlotkowski, Director; Dr. Jim Ostrow, Director of Research; and Ms. Amy Kenworthy, Administrative Coordinator — of the Bentley Service Learning Project at Bentley College ◆ Dr. Bill Denton, Professor of Educational Leadership; and Dr. Beryl Mitchel, Coordinator of Community Services — at Clark-Atlanta University ◆ Dr. Jim Scarratt, Director; and Dr. Gaia Mica, Associate Director — of the INVST Program at the University of Colorado ◆ Ms. Deborah White, Director of the Student Activities Center — at Eastern Tennessee State University ◆ Dr. Judy Rauner, Director of the Office of Community Service-Learning — at the University of San Diego ◆ Ms. Kim Johnson-Bogart, Director; and Ms. Shelly Fields, Coordinator of Special Projects and Students — of the Edward E. Carlson Leadership and Public Service Office at the University of Washington ◆

Mr. James Keith and Dr. Jackie Schmidt-Posner assisted by conducting student interviews ◆ Dr. Cheryl Keen critiqued an early draft of the interview protocol ◆ As a part of a presentation in our Adult Learning Class, Vanderbilt graduate student Mr. Jeff Kenyon shared with us the Grinch's moment of critical reflection.

A very special thanks to Ms. Sharon Powell, our project coordinator, who effectively coordinated and conducted student interviews, and coded transcripts. Thank you also to Ms. Heather Gard who preceded Sharon as project coordinator and was instrumental in getting the process launched. Without their work, the project could not have been completed.

And of course, this project would not have been possible without the support of the Corporation for National Service.

Janet Eyler
Dwight E. Giles, Jr.
Angela Schmiede

TABLE of CONTENTS

Chapter 3
DIFFERENT WAYS TO REFLECT AND LEARN
PAGE 47

Chapter 4
PUTTING REFLECTION INTO ACTION
PAGE 61

Appendices
PAGE 161

INTRODUCTION

THE STORY OF THIS PROJECT

"*And I think that's what this reflection does, it really challenges people to do something that they're not used to doing. Therefore, they see things in a different way and are able to analyze it or get something out of it that they normally wouldn't have.*"

— University of San Diego student

THE POWER OF "THE 'AH HA' MOMENT"

During the past few years, while conducting another service-learning research project, we were continually reminded of the importance of critical reflection in service-learning. As we interviewed students, listened to their stories, assembled focus groups, and read survey questionnaires, we became increasingly aware that important moments of insight and intellectual and personal transformation *were* occurring for students in service-learning courses and programs. As teachers in the tradition of experiential education, we were not surprised by evidence of such moments of transformation; it only echoed our own experiences as practitioners. We had witnessed the power of "the 'Ah ha!' moment" with the students in our courses and service-learning programs. What did impress us, however, was the frequency with which students themselves related stories of the power of critical reflection.

A STUDENT'S TESTIMONY

The event which led to the eventual crystallization of this project occurred in March of 1994, when one of us attended the Community Service-Learning conference at the University of Michigan. One of the opening speakers, Jennifer Bastress, related how after extensive community service in high school, she came to college without any experience of asking "why?" or of doing any critical reflection about the causes and solutions of the social problems to which she was volunteering her time. She confessed to the conference attendees, "I just didn't get it" (Bastress, 1996, p.22).

As a result of her subsequent involvement in service-learning projects at the University of Michigan, however, Jen developed the capacity to link her service to the broader questions and the issues she was studying in her classes. As she noted, "I learned what it meant to look at an issue and break it down, to see the inter-connectedness and the complexity of

"I learned what it meant to look at an issue and break it down, to see the inter-connectedness and the complexity of an issue such as homelessness, to brainstorm and initiate strategies that addressed root causes and to avoid slapping a 'band-aid' on a symptom.."

an issue such as homelessness, to brainstorm and initiate strategies that addressed root causes and to avoid slapping a 'band-aid' on a symptom.... I learned that my work with the community, and the critical thinking skills I was using, could become part of my classes in the larger academic community. I could finally tie what I was learning from my text books and lectures to what was happening in my community and my world." (Bastress, 1996, p. 22.)

Later during the conference, we discussed service-learning research with Goodwin Liu, who at that time was the Senior Program Officer for Higher Education at the Corporation for National and Community Service. When he asked how research could help practice in service-learning, we replied that we knew that there was a wealth of stories — like Jennifer's — out there: stories of service-learning students who eventually "got it" as a result of critical reflection.

We noted that with the exception of Harry Silcox's book, (1993) very little literature on reflection in service-learning existed, and we had not been able to find *any* that was empirical or research-based. Out of that discussion, and several that followed, this project was born: a research-based initiative to examine students' experiences of critical reflection. We hoped to help the field hear the students' stories, be inspired by them, and learn from them what types of reflection had helped students "get it".

GATHERING STORIES OF REFLECTION

It was clear to us from the very beginning that the only research methodology that was appropriate for this project was to use in-depth, personal, semi-structured interviews. No other data gathering method was capable of capturing the richness of the experience while providing a consistent approach to inquiring about modes of reflection. After several pilot interviews, we settled on an interview guide consisting of five basic areas of questioning (*See Appendix D for interview guide*). Each interview was tape recorded and lasted an average of about 45 minutes. Interviewers were trained to probe for specific examples of helpful reflection experiences and techniques. Interviewees also filled out a brief service-learning history sheet that was used to gather data on background characteristics and previous experiences.

After conducting our pilot interviews at Vanderbilt and the University of Tennessee, we selected six colleges and universities from the list of Corporation grantees to participate in the study: Bentley College, The University of San Diego, The University of Colorado, East Tennessee State University, Clark-Atlanta University, and the University of Washington. While we could not *begin* to represent the diversity of the types of higher education in such a small sample, we selected colleges and universities that varied in size, geographic location, type of service-learning program, history and traditions (historically black, private, public, liberal arts, pre-professional, etc.).

We interviewed a total of 67 students: 60 of the students represented the traditional student age range of 19-22, but seven students were older. The gender ratio among participants was 45 women and 22 men, which is consistent with existing evidence about the gender ratio among participants in most service programs nationwide. Of the 67 students, 48 were Caucasian, 11 were African-American, five were Asian-American, and three were Latino.

While we were primarily interested in structured reflection that occurs in the classroom, we also wanted to explore reflection activities that occur in co-curricular programs, as well as self-directed reflection; we therefore selected a sampling of 46 students who had taken specific courses with service-learning options and 21 who had previously been involved only in co-curricular service projects. The data presented in this text focus primarily on the students who had the more structured reflective experiences.

The project's data analysis involved entering the transcribed interviews into a word processing data base. We then used qualitative analysis software (Ethnograph) to perform content analysis and to code themes and types of reflection. After a preliminary analysis of the types of reflection mentioned, we refined our coding categories and settled on the four main categories presented in Chapter 3 and used to categorize the Reflection Activities in Chapter 4.

As we developed a coding system we began with outcome categories used in some of our earlier work with service-learning (Eyler & Giles, 1993) and with Harry Silcox's (1993) matrix linking types of reflection and outcomes. We revised these matrices by dropping some types and adding others that matched our data, thus resulting in the 24 cell matrix that forms the organizational structure of Chapter 4. (See Page 65). We were particularly interested in organizing the data according to specific modes of reflection and the accompanying outcomes because we wanted to see which modes of reflection were most useful for different outcomes.

THE DESIGN OF THIS GUIDE

We have designed and organized this guide as a resource for anyone seeking to use critical reflection in service-learning: among these individuals we hope to include teachers, students, program leaders, and community agency representatives. The purpose of the guide is to draw upon student testimony of successful reflection and to translate their stories into practice. To the best of our knowledge this guide is the first and only resource currently available on reflection that is based directly on student experiences. It is not meant to supplant but to *supplement* existing resources on theories of reflection and surveys of techniques drawn from program materials.

The nature of the student interviews of course meant that students described reflection activities with varying degrees of specificity. The collection of reflection activities included in Chapter 4, therefore, includes some with detailed facilitation tips and numerous variations while others include more cursory descriptions. We have drawn upon some program materials to supplement student descriptions, particularly in the case study in Chapter 4, which is designed to model sequencing of activities. These examples are included, however, only based on the responses of the students whom we interviewed.

We have also field tested our preliminary findings through the Corporation for National Service's five regional workshops, in which we participated as part of our technical assistance grant. Our audience consisted of service-learning practitioners who were also Corporation grantees. The reactions to these workshops and the techniques we piloted there were overwhelmingly positive. From those workshop participants, we also received many suggestions that have helped to refine and strengthen our final product.

THE BASIC IDEA

This guide is intended to be a practical resource to assist in developing reflection activities for service-learning courses, programs, and other forms of experience-based education. It is interactive by design and should foster active engagement on the part of the reader, through both the nature of its content and the accessibility of its structure.

WHAT'S COMING UP

Much of the text consists of stories and personal testimony — told in the exact words of students involved in critical reflection and service-learning. This student commentary is both the source of practical suggestions provided in this guide, and the element that brings the theoretical concept of reflection alive, for us and — we hope — for you. It is our belief that you will find in their voices much of what service-learning practitioners need most: the inspiration to do what you do, the supporting evidence to convince colleagues and administrators of the value of reflective service-learning, and the "how-to's" to plan reflection that will be meaningful and effective for your own program or classroom.

WHAT TO DO WITH IT ALL

Read this guide from beginning to end. Or, if you prefer a less linear approach, use the notes on the facing page to do a "fast find" for specific information. Check the Matrix on page 65 to locate a certain type of reflection activity — Chapter 4 is filled with step-by-step guidelines to the activities that our interviewees recommended. Or flip through the student quotations (especially in Chapter 2) for material to support particular approaches to reflection.

EXPERIMENT AS YOU GO

Each chapter begins with a suggested exercise to help you be a reflective practitioner in the very process of learning to promote reflective service-learning among others.

WHAT DO *you* NEED?

...to reflect on using service-learning in your classes or programs?	GO TO..	...the 'reflecting on service-learning' activities at the beginning of each chapter.
...to convince colleagues or administrators that service-learning is important to student learning outcomes?	GO TO..	...Chapter 1 — for critical elements of reflection ...and Chapter 2 — for student reflections on the value of reflection and service-learning. ...and Appendices — for further references
...to find out what students value about service-learning experiences?	GO TO..	...Chapter 2 — for student reflections on the value of reflection and service-learning.
...to develop varied instructional activities around service?	GO TO..	...Chapter 3 — for principles of writing, reading, telling and doing. ...and Chapter 4 — for the matrix and sample assignments.
...to adapt activities for students with different learning styles?	GO TO..	...Chapter 3 — for a guide to selecting activities.
...to create an appropriate sequence for reflection activities in your class?	GO TO..	....Chapter 1 — for a description of the "4 C's" ...and Chapter 4 — for a case study in sequencing reflection activities.
...to develop reflection activities for a student group when community service is not part of a class?	GO TO..	...Chapter 4 — for a variety of appropriate activities. In particular, try *Reflection Activities for Large Group Discussion.* (page 141) or *Encouraging Informal Discussion* (page 128)
...to identify other resources for planning service-learning classes and reflection activities?	GO TO..	...the Appendices and the list of References at the close of each chapter.

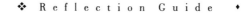

INTRODUCTION REFERENCES

Bastress, J. "Students as agents of social change." In Galura, J., Howard, J., Waterhouse, D, and Ross, R. (eds.). *Praxis III: Voices in Dialogue.* Ann Arbor, Michigan: OCSL Publications, 1996.

Eyler, J. and Giles, D.E., Jr. "What We Know. What We Need to Know. Directions and Issues in Field Based Education." Atlanta: *American Educational Research Association*, 1993.

Silcox, H.C. *A How-To Guide to Reflection: Adding Cognitive Learning to Community Service Programs.* Philadelphia, Pennsylvania: Brighton Press, 1993.

CHAPTER 1
REFLECTION AND SERVICE-LEARNING

And the Grinch, with his grinch-feet ice-cold in the snow, Stood puzzling and puzzling: "How could it be so?.... And he puzzled three hours, till his puzzler was sore. Then the Grinch thought of something he hadn't before.

— Dr. Seuss, *How the Grinch Stole Christmas*!

CRITICAL REFLECTION IN EVERYDAY LIFE

As this excerpt from the tale of the Grinch illustrates, we all confront moments in everyday life when we must stop and reflect on what we have experienced. This is particularly true when we are puzzled or surprised by our experiences or when something happens that we cannot explain using the explanations that seemed to work in the past. Sometimes, when we face this type of dissonance between what we know and what we experience, we need to be encouraged and assisted — either by another individual or by a thoughtfully constructed process that we can follow — in our efforts to puzzle and to ask reflective questions. This additional challenge and support is especially crucial on those occasions when it would seem much easier to ignore the dissonance that confronts us, or when we might be inclined, if left alone, to apply an old and familiar – but often inadequate – framework to explain what we have experienced in the most comfortable manner possible. Critical reflection is a process specifically structured to help examine the frameworks that we use to interpret experience; critical reflection pushes us to step outside of the old and familiar and to reframe our questions and our conclusions in innovative and more effective terms.

Critical reflection does not, however, require particularly technical training. Rather, the view that emerges from the

Before reading this chapter, take a moment to ponder your own theories of learning:

1. What basic assumptions about how students learn shape your choices about class assignments and activities?

2. How do you think community service contributes to the learning process?

3. If you were going to give a friend advice about the basic principles that make for effective service-learning, what would you say?

This chapter discusses key elements of effective reflection as identified by students. As you read, compare your own learning assumptions with those outlined in the chapter.

students whom we interviewed in this study is that, when applied intentionally, the basic reflective and puzzling techniques that help us make sense of everyday life form the core of the very same techniques that enable students to derive meaningful learning from the experience of service.

An additional dimension of critical reflection emerges from the student voices represented within this text: the form of reflection that goes beyond the everyday questioning of and wondering about events. It is the critical questioning of why things are and the attempt to fully understand the root causes of observable events and behaviors. This depth of critical reflection grows out of the instinctual reflective process but must be cultivated purposefully as a habit of the mind.

The effectiveness of critical reflection on this more complex level does depend on someone taking responsibility for making it happen; and the prompting of a peer or the guidance of a program leader can be indispensable. In this guide our student interviewees present insights into the art of effective teaching and learning, and methods to pose the appropriate question at a strategic point in time in order to create *the teachable moment.*

THE ROLE OF REFLECTION IN LINKING SERVICE TO LEARNING

"Service, combined with learning, adds value to each and transforms both." (Honnet and Poulsen, 1989).

This central tenet of service-learning is expressed in the preamble to the *Principles of Good Practice in Combining Service and Learning.* In practice it is critical reflection, as recognized in the 1993 National and Community Service Trust Act, that provides the transformative link between the action of *serving* and the ideas and understanding of *learning.*

HOW DO WE LEARN FROM EXPERIENCE?

The question of how to make experience educative is one that has challenged experiential educators for much of this century. In that service-learning relies on the experience of service, it shares this question with other forms of experiential education. In his posing of this question, John Dewey (1933), asserted that the core of the learning experience must be a project (in this case service-learning) or experience from which the student can draw conclusions about the world. Dewey proposed four criteria that were necessary for "projects to be truly educative":

1. Must generate interest.

2. Must be worthwhile intrinsically.

3. Must present problems that awaken new curiosity and create a demand for information.

4. Must cover a considerable time span and be capable of fostering development over time.

THE ROLE OF REFLECTIVE THINKING

In addition, however, Dewey held that ***reflective thinking*** was the key to making experience educative. Reflective thinking provides the bridge between the world of observed and experienced facts with ideas. As Dewey pointed out, reflective thinking is a part of the larger process of reflective activity. Dewey saw reflective activity as having five phases:

1. Suggestion

The inhibition of tendency to act, to pursue whatever suggestion arises from the situation by stopping to consider more than one course of action.

2. Intellectualization

The definition of a problem and the raising of questions about the nature of the problem and possible solutions.

3. The Hypothesis

The development of the guiding idea based on observation and previous knowledge.

4. Reasoning

The development of the hypothesis by applying knowledge and by developing the linkages in the sequence of ideas.

5. Testing the Hypothesis in Action

The verification through further observation or experimentation in which the problem is solved or a new problem is presented.

Reflection leads to understanding, which in turn leads to more informed action. Effective reflection leads to a better understanding of social problems *and* to the quest for better solutions. Dewey also pointed out that critical reflection leads to the synthesis of old and new knowledge — including new ways of understanding and solving problems. Part of this process involves asking new questions. (Dewey, 1933). Like the Grinch, service-learning students often have to ask "Why?" and "What else?" as they confront the realities of social and community issues.

Following Dewey, other educational theorists have pursued the questions of how reflection links thinking and acting. One of the most frequently mentioned theories is David Kolb's model of the experiential learning cycle (1984). Kolb argues that we move in a cycle from the concrete experience to a new level of knowing that we then test in action, thus beginning the cycle again. The cycle — involving action, reflection, conceptual knowledge (ideas) based on the prior action and reflection, and finally, experimental action — is illustrated in further detail in Chapter 3.

PUTTING THEORY TO USE

While the actual practice of reflection is an entirely natural process of the human mind and spirit, such theorists and Kolb and Dewey advocate a very purposeful process of Reflection — reflection with an **"R"** — to maximize the effectiveness of the learning cycle. Students interviewed also stressed the importance of informal reflection — with an **"r"** — which takes place on an individual basis during unstructured personal time, or through casual conversations with friends, relatives and coworkers. Students commented on the need to balance this informal reflection with more formalized critical thinking. While a number of student quotations in Chapter 2 deal with the effect of informal reflection time, the remainder of this guide inevitably addresses the more thorough and intentional process of engaging in some sort of structured Reflection: students were simply able to provide specific suggestions mainly for *structured* activities that ensure that Reflective Action and the Kolb learning cycle actually occur.

David Kolb's (1984) cycle provided the theoretical foundation for one of the most common techniques for reflective thinking: The "What? So What? Now What?" model of reflection, popularized largely by the Campus Opportunity Outreach League (COOL). These simple but powerful questions direct the flow of reflective thought, from the descriptive phase ("What?") through the interpretive and emotive phase ("So What?"), and finally into the active phase ("Now What?"). (See chapter 4, page 139) (See also Axt 1994; Willette et al, 1994.) This basic model moves the learner from considering the concrete experience to discerning the meaning of the event and then to applying the conclusions to plans for continued action. This simple model neatly illustrates Dewey's linking of action and reflection as the key to learning from experience.

The experiences of the students we encountered through this study emphasize the crucial role of critical reflection in the process of service-learning. A comparison of the responses of students who had been involved in critical reflection with those who had not, found that the students who had not been engaged in programs with reflective components were most likely to focus on the affective, the personal and the empathic dimensions of the experience. The students who were engaged in critical reflection incorporated these dimensions of the experience in their commentary, but were much more likely to report also a better sense of application of ideas to social problems and a transformed understanding of the problem and issues surrounding it. We are persuaded that reflection is the glue that holds service and learning together to provide educative experiences.

THE 4 C'S: PRINCIPLES OF REFLECTION

The opening section of this chapter noted that reflection is not an overly technical process, despite its importance in fostering learning outcomes and new forms of understanding and action. Having said that, we must emphasize that there are some common and necessary elements of successful reflection; it need not be a difficult process, but it does need to be a purposeful and strategic process.

After analyzing our interview data, we reflected on the common themes or principles that were present across all of the forms of reflection reported by the students we interviewed. From this process emerged the four C's of reflection; it is our conclusion that effective critical reflection is:

Continuous • Connected • Challenging • Contextualized

Continuous Reflection

The most effective reflection is Continuous on two critical levels. First and most important, students commented that critical reflection must be an ongoing part of a learner's education and service involvement over the course of his or her educational career. Facilitating this process may not be as difficult as one might think, however — early short term direct service experiences often led to later, more intense service involvement.

Continuous reflection allows the student to continue formulating new ways to view the world, using four or more years' worth of service-learning experience as material for observation, reflection and experimentation — following the Kolb Cycle with a commitment to long-term reflective action and a growing awareness and experience that leads to more complex service as well.

On another level, reflection should maintain an especially coherent continuity over the course of each event or experience. Continuous reflection includes reflection *before* the experience, *during* the experience and *after* the experience.

Student interviewees often mentioned reflective preparation for an experience as critical to getting the most out of each experience. Most reflection occurring during the experience was geared toward problem-solving and proposing immediate action to enhance the effectiveness of the experience. Reflection after the service tended to focus on evaluating the meaning of the service, integrating new understandings into previous knowledge, and planning future action.

> *"... I think the main thing that helps is that all of us in the organization, we sit down and talk about the different problems... We do it every Sunday... sit down and talk about the different things."*

"*I think the main thing that helps is that all of us in the organization, we sit down and talk about the different problems — and also, you can't find the solutions to problems in books, you can get a basic understanding, maybe - but until you deal with the problem and have to focus on it, you don't know how to respond to that. So, a lot of times it helps to sit down in a group. We do it every Sunday... sit down and talk about the different things.*"

— Bentley College student

Connected Reflection

Connected reflection links service to the intellectual and academic pursuits of the students. As illustrated in Chapter 2, this connectedness should operate on two levels. Service experiences illustrate theories and concepts, bringing statistics to life and making academics real and vivid. Through classroom work, in turn, students begin to develop conceptual frameworks that explain service experiences. And intensive service-learning experiences can also serve as capstone courses to integrate concepts across the curriculum. Academic pursuits add a "big picture" context to the personal encounters of each isolated service experience and help students to search for causes and solutions to social problems.

The synthesis of action and thought results from connected reflection. Interviewees repeatedly expressed the importance of integrating what they were doing in their service with what they were studying. As Jennifer's speech cited at the beginning of the Introduction illustrates, the result of connected reflection is not only more effective service and more effective learning, but also a sense of empowerment and personal growth that inspired in many students a commitment to both their current service and continued service involvement.

"...We constantly take real life situations and apply it to what's in the book so that we can intermingle the two and come up with solid conclusions for problems that are relevant..."

"*Basically what she does is she opens the arena for discussion. What we basically do is we take a particular problem and we relate it to information from the text. For example, the Wednesday past, we talked about class management. There's a lady in the class that seemed to be having a problem with a student that constantly wanted to disrupt the class. So, what we did was we looked at the chapter in our text which dealt with classroom management and we figured out that maybe if she was to give that student more work, maybe then that problem would subside. Or maybe if she pulled that student aside and worked with him individually again, that could eradicate that problem. So, we constantly take real life situations and apply it to what's in the book so that we can intermingle the two and come up with solid conclusions for problems that are relevant.*"

— Clark Atlanta University Student

Challenging Reflection

One of the most critical components of effective reflection is also one that some service-learning practitioners find most difficult to implement: the practice of challenging students to engage issues in a more critical way. Challenging reflection requires intervention on the part of a teacher or colleague who is prepared to pose questions and propose unfamiliar or even uncomfortable ideas for consideration by the learner.

Our students reported that challenging reflection pushed them to think in new ways, to develop alternative explanations for experiences and observations, and to question their original perceptions of events and issues.

The role of the teacher or facilitator in implementing challenging reflection, however, requires that he or she balance the process of challenging the learner while simultaneously offering support. It is crucial that a "safe space" — where learners feel confident that their contributions, backgrounds and feelings will be respected and appreciated — be maintained between facilitator and learner, and within any reflection group.

In this way, students reported, the nurturing and affirming aspects of reflection, which engender personal growth, also create an environment in which a teacher, a peer, or a community partner can pose the *challenging* reflection that students said produces new understanding, raises new questions, and moves towards new frameworks for problem solving.

"... She asked the right questions and she said, I need more research, I need more research and have you thought about this?..."

"One of my teachers made me or forced me to do a... directed kind of study.... I wrote a paper for a class on the homeless and she wasn't an expert on the homeless but as a good teacher, she asked the right questions and she said, I need more research, I need more research and have you thought about this? So it was just those little red marks on a paper that made me go back and find an article and then, you know, that really makes sense. So I think it was the process of researching a paper that I learned more."
— University of Tennessee student

Contextualized Reflection

"...When you apply what you're learning that's the way you really learn it... If you don't practice it, you're not going to learn it..."

Contextualized reflection is appropriate for the setting and context of a particular service-learning course or program; the environment and method of reflection corresponds in a meaningful way to the topics and experiences that form the material for reflection. Immersion in an authentic community experience provides a rich context for learning, adding relevance to academic exploration. Reflection, when it is purposefully implemented in an appropriate and meaningful context, adds to the richness of the synthesis between thinking and doing.

One key element of context is degree of formality involved in any given reflection activity.. A service-learning course will generally lend itself to structured assignments and fairly formal discussion, whereas a service-learning experience that takes place outside of any academic setting ends well with an informal reflection circle. If the reflection setting feels too formalized for the context, it runs the risk of being experienced, as one student put it, "too much like school".

In addition, the proximity of the reflection session to the community in which students are working lends a strong flavor to any reflection session. A discussion of relations between a college campus and its surrounding community might gain depth and vitality if conducted off campus with community members participating as well. Other topics of consideration — theoretical concepts, or personal frustrations with events or individuals, for example — can be better served by some distance from the community.

Many students mentioned the same reflection questions being used but presented in oral or written modes, their format depending on the context of the issue and the situation. Many of the students recalled details of both the context and the mode of their most helpful reflection experiences.

"I firmly believe that when you apply what you're learning that's the way you really learn it. A perfect example is of learning another language. You can go to class and you can learn the verbs and the subjunctives and all those technical things, but if you don't practice it, you're not going to learn it. And the only way to learn another language is to practice it and ideally go to the other country and spend some time there to really apply it. But that's where the learning takes place. That's why I believe so strongly in this. Because everybody is benefiting from this service, whether it be the agency... [or] the student."

— University of San Diego student

CONCLUSION

Over the course of this study, certain themes have appeared repeatedly as critical factors in effective reflective activity. The best reflection is **_Continuous_** in time frame, **_Connected_** to the "big picture" information provided by academic pursuits, **_Challenging_** to assumptions and complacency, and **_Contextualized_** in terms of design and setting. These 4 C's form the foundation of any meaningful reflective experience; as you use this guide to develop reflection activities, we suggest that you ask how you can make sure that the 4 C's are implemented in adapting the techniques and lessons illustrated in this guide.

CHAPTER 1 REFERENCES

Axt, D. *Site Leader Survival Manual.* Nashville: Break Away: The Alternative Break Connection, 1994.

Dewey, J. *How We Think.* Boston: Heath, 1933.

Dewey, J. *Experience and Education.* New York: Collier Books, 1938.

Honnet, E.P. & Poulsen, S. *Principles of Good Practice for Combining Service and Learning.* (Wingspread Special Report). Racine, Wisconsin: The Johnson Foundation, Inc., 1989

Kolb, D.A. *Experiential Learning: Experience as the Source of Learning and Development.* Englewood Cliffs, New Jersey: Prentice-Hall, 1984.

Seuss, Dr. *How the Grinch Stole Christmas.* New York: Random House, 1957

Willette, Z., Magevney, M., & Mann, L. *Curriculum-Based Alternative Breaks: The Manual.* Nashville: Break Away: The Alternative Break Connection, 1994

CHAPTER

STUDENT VOICES
ON THE VALUE OF REFLECTION

"All those things that we had to do for the service-learning. Each one successively helped me to pull together what I'd learned. As you're going along, you're not really seeing what you're learning every minute. But, when you have to pull it all together and really think about it, I think it helped me realize what had taken place."

— University of San Diego student

Service itself was an educative experience for many of our students. It would be hard to imagine a situation more likely to embody the key elements of educative experience identified by Dewey than a service project. The students are doing work that is 'intrinsically worthwhile' and is 'capable of fostering development over time'. There is a good deal of evidence in these interviews that the experiences 'generate interest' and 'present problems that awaken new curiosity and a demand for new information.' (Giles & Eyler, 1994)

For many of the students, the experience provoked spontaneous reflection. They found themselves thinking about the people with whom they worked and situations they encountered. In some cases, they sought out or were challenged by others — roommates, friends, family — to reflect on the meaning of their experience. Reflection is not limited to formal or structured reflection, but those who were involved in service-learning classes with structured reflection did tend to differ in what they reported about the effects of their experience from those whose service was co-curricular.

This Chapter focuses on what students believe they have gained from reflecting on service. Before you read the chapter, consider this... Think about classes you have taught that incorporate community service:

1. Did the process of incorporating service into your class change the way you think about yourself as a teacher?

2. Did you gain new insight into the subject matter by helping your students combine service & learning?

3. Did combining service with learning change the way you view the process of teaching & learning?

If you found yourself changed by teaching classes which involved students in service, your experiences parallel those of the students we interviewed. Many students report that the service-learning experience contributed to personal growth, to their understanding of course work, and to the way in which they view social issues. In this chapter, students share these insights in their own words.

Most students reported that the service experience had an impact on the way they felt about themselves and about their feelings of connectedness to others and to community. The affective power of this experience is dramatic, and this affective power can provide an impetus moving students into both further service involvement and a search for knowledge leading to cognitive outcomes.

Students who were involved in service-learning courses which combined structured reflection with service were more likely to talk about what they had learned about social issues, about the subject matter of their courses and also how their perspective about community problems had changed. Service is a powerful experience for most; service coupled with formal opportunities for reflection appears to help students integrate the service experience with their understanding of their society.

This chapter shares the insights of our students in their own words. The comments have been selected to illustrate the multiple outcomes of service and reflection on service identified by these 67 college and university students. The first section of commentary relates to the motivational power of service-learning. The attraction of service-learning for students increases as they participate, dramatically increasing the chance that they will continue their involvement and benefit increasingly from the outcomes of service-learning involvement.

The subsequent sections address those very outcomes — six core outcomes of service-learning mentioned in the student interviews. These outcomes — Personal Development, Connecting to Others, Citizenship Development, Understanding, Application, and Reframing — form the structure of the Reflection Activity Matrix on Page 65, which serves as an index to the reflection activities detailed in all of Chapter 4.

Service-Learning Motivates Students to Learn

One of the qualities of an educative experience is that it leads students to want to learn more about an issue. The power of even a single service experience to cause students to question and want to learn more is impressive. Central to the impact of service-learning on enhanced understanding is this link between passion and curiosity. And the reflection activities may add to the motivational value of the experience by helping students see the importance of their contributions.

PASSION ABOUT LEARNING MORE

"I can honestly say that I've learned more in this last year in community service than I probably have learned in all four years of college. I have learned so much. Maybe because I found something that I'm really passionate about and it makes you care more to learn about it — and to get involved and to do more. You're not just studying to take a test and forget about it. You're learning and the experiences we have are staying with us. It's not cram for a test the night before... I know when I take a test I just want to get it over with and that doesn't happen with community service, it stays with you."

— University of San Diego student

"...I felt like we, the people who did the service, were a little more able to discuss in the classroom. ...We were all doing basically the same kind of subject matter. Like when we had discussions that pertained to that we were all — it was all very personal to us. And we felt a lot about it and said a lot about it too."

— University of Washington Student

CURIOSITY ABOUT ISSUES

"I had a lot of questions after I did my paper, but that was too late, 'cause the class was over and I wished the class was all year long... I kind of wanted solutions which is a ridiculous thing to ask for, because it's impossible. And I saw [my service program] as a form of a solution to these problems we were talking about. It just made me want to understand more and more the structure and why these people are there."

—University of Washington student

"And no one else felt comfortable [assisting a disabled homeless man with his meal] and so I said I would do it. And it took me a long time to do it. And most everyone was gone when I left. I took about an hour to feed the gentleman. It was a great experience for me. It totally changed — I wanted to know why these people were on the street and I wanted to know who was helping them. So, when I got into Bentley I started to get involved. Right there that one incident changed me, I wanted to help people."

— Bentley College student

"*It just made me want to understand more and more the structure and why these people are there.*"

"*My service has raised a lot of questions and they've been raised again in the sociology class. What is a social problem — and it totally depends on who's in power. Like who's defining social problems. In the 1950s or whatever, whites didn't think racism was a social problem. And so it totally depends on what point in history you are and who you are and where you're at.*"　　　　　　　　　　　　　　　— University of Washington student

"*Questions that I wanted to ask were, 'Why in the world would a 12-year-old be involved in a situation like this? What kind of family does he come from? What kind of neighborhood? Why, if it is bad, is it like that in the first place? What could happen to improve the situation? If the school is not providing a good education, why is that? How come the money is not going there?... Why is it that everyone in the courtroom is so mechanical with no feeling? Was it because they had seen this a million times or that they didn't care?'*"　　　　　　　　　　　　— Vanderbilt University student

REFLECTION VALIDATING THE EXPERIENCE

"*And I think [writing in a journal] makes you reflect on the experience and how much time you put into it and how much work it was, and how much time you spent thinking, it makes it seem — it sort of validates the experience.*"

— University of Washington student

"*With community service-learning you see a broader picture by watching things play out instead of just volunteering. It is a more structured environment. You have a purpose when you go into it. I'm not sure how other classes are, but ours has a purpose to connect their lives with public policy.*"　　　　　　　— University of San Diego student

Service-Learning Aids Personal Development

Students in college are struggling with questions about who they are and what they wish to make of their lives. Service challenges their assumptions about self and provokes thought about themselves and their future. Opportunities to reflect on the personal meaning of service experiences — whether created informally through interactions with peers or in structured settings — may enhance the power of this process. Students felt that their service helped make them more confident, compassionate and less prejudiced people and to know themselves better. The power of service to stimulate personal reflection was clear in student comments.

SELF-CONFIDENCE AND MATURITY

"*I think it helps in so many different ways – not just about learning, but it helps you to become more assured of yourself, more self esteem. It makes you more responsible because in some situations you have to take control of what you're doing... I've learned so much leadership in the past two semesters than I've had in all of my high school. ...Now I'm not afraid to go and talk in front of 30 or something. I'm not afraid to take control and be sure of what I'm saying, because I've become an expert in certain areas and I know about that. It helps your self esteem so much and you feel like you're getting something accomplished and you feel like you're helping others and it's the best feeling you can ever get.*"

— University of San Diego student

"*In class, they're just statistics. So many people are homeless, so many... killed by gang warfare... blah, blah blah. But, if you're actually out there... you know their names and you know who they are...*"

"*I want everyone to have that kind of experience, to do community service. And a lot of it's grunt work. A lot of it's harder than [regular classes] — reading a book and taking a multiple choice test for me is a lot easier than going into an organization and getting dumped on and feeling different dynamics of working with people. But that's to me what life is all about – working with people. All those experiences, positive and negative and like failed fund-raisers, they all add up and make me feel like I'm a much more well rounded person and able to really exist and survive in this society.*"

— University of Colorado student

COMPASSION AND PRE-JUDGMENT

"*I think I have a lot more compassion [than non-service peers]. In class, they're just statistics. So many people are homeless, so many people are being killed by gang warfare... blah, blah, blah. But, if you're actually out there, it's not so many people, it's lots of human beings that you know and you know their names and you know who they are.*"

— University of Washington student

"*I've learned not to judge people, I think. That's the most important thing that I've learned. I can only say I think I did before. And now, working with people who are not as fortunate as I am, makes me realize that they're just the same as I am.*"

— Bentley College student

KNOWING MYSELF

"*Each time I do a new service, I see the importance of that channel of service. And that all comes together to, hopefully when I get out of school, know basically what I want to do.*"

— Vanderbilt University student

"*...It's given me an opportunity to have a personal relationship with some people in my school that I wouldn't have had otherwise...*"

"*I think it taught me where my buttons are. What things I can tolerate, what things I can't tolerate. I want to work in the community, but that doesn't mean I want to work directly with the kids. There's other avenues. And I think in trying that out, I realized - this is exactly what I wanted to do – or no, I don't like this part. So I think that was important on a reflective basis for me to figure out what I want to do.*"

— Bentley College student

Service-Learning Helps Students Connect to Others

Many students feel isolated and lost in large colleges and universities; this craving for a sense of belonging is directly associated with student attrition. Several students identified service — particularly service as a part of the curriculum — as a way that they bridged this gap in their college lives. While any community service activity brings people into contact with others, the reflection activities of service-learning classes join the emotional power of doing *real work for real people* in the field with the structure provided by academic tasks.

Serving and then completing assignments together helps students connect with their peers and with faculty members, establish bonds with people on campus and off whom they might not otherwise get to know, feel a part of their institution and improve their learning. Here is how students describe it:

"...I've had to deal with situations that I never would have been confronted with if I hadn't been a volunteer..."

LINKS WITH PEERS & FACULTY

"I have learned to work with people... an important skill... This is a big school, there are 25,000 students here and in most of my classes I don't know my professor, he has no idea who I am... so it's given me an opportunity to have a personal relationship with some people in my school that I wouldn't have had otherwise... like-minded people who care about these issues and want to make a difference."

— University of Colorado student

"It was great because whenever you go into a new school you wonder what people think about what you are doing. And here, in this class we had people who were in sororities, fraternities, athletes, people that were really into academics. But for once a week, every week for two years, we all got together and went to the homeless shelter. Which is great because you have people that are from all over- California, Boston, Montana, Maine - all had different perspectives - all had different experiences and we brought it together and we got to come together every week and deal with that. We would end up driving there

talking about what's going to happen and then coming back, we're all having our own focus group every week or reflection groups every week just for ourselves."

— Bentley College student

LINKS WITH DIVERSE OTHERS

"I suppose I learned about real life. That's the only way I can put it. I've encountered people that I never would have met if I hadn't been a volunteer. I've had to deal with situations that I never would have been confronted with if I hadn't been a volunteer. And I've been able to forge friendships with people that I never would have met if I hadn't worked. For instance... I worked all summer with one of the students and she was so quiet and so shy and I had such a hard time reaching her. And then I was home for spring break and I was watching the St. Patrick's Day parade in our little tiny town and she came running across the street and hugged me. And I thought — wow I never would have talked to her - we never would have met if it hadn't been for the experience."

— University of San Diego student

".. It has enhanced what I learned in books... it's made it stick and click for me."

"A lot of the things we study in classes that have to do with cultural diversity are really important before going out and doing service... when you go and do service, there's such a diverse population that needs service. That sort of information, just knowledge about how different people work is really important."

— University of Colorado student

LINKS TO THE INSTITUTION

"I didn't know why I was here at this university until I joined [this program]. I felt like I was lost and I was just a number and I didn't really want this to be my life and I had never really heard of service-learning. Then education really started to make sense for me... It has enhanced what I learned in books, not just memorizing before a test, but it's made it stick and click for me."

— University of Colorado student

"One of the reasons I came to Bentley is because of the service-learning. And it's a wonderful college, but I got into better ones – but I wanted to go here because of the service-learning programs. And I love it 'cause I love the service. It's one of the main reasons I came here; it's made a big difference."

— Bentley College student

"...You're actually working with those people you're talking about in class: it makes it seem much more real and much more urgent to do something ..."

Service-Learning Helps Students Develop Commitment to Active Citizenship

Part of the development of a mature identity is the development of a sense of self as a contributing part of the community. One effect of service-learning that students identified was their growing sense of responsibility to do something about community problems. This stemmed from their growing understanding of the systemic nature of social problems and their empathy and identification with those with whom they worked in their service projects. Classes which stressed the root causes of social problems and helped students make those links also led to heightened commitment to social change. Students talked about their sense of self as citizen:

CITIZENSHIP IN THE COMMUNITY

"I would never have really truly understood these issues – like homelessness... it is learning a larger scale of these issues. Instead of just seeing myself working with the shelter or a few kids, I guess I have a picture of myself as part of a larger community working with these issues. I don't feel isolated. I've learned the importance of community when you are working with the social arena." — University of Colorado student

"[Service] is an integral part of who I am. It really is my basis for how I live my life and so to ask me to stop it would be to ask me to stop living... in the face of how overwhelming the problems are and how it seems as though our contributions are so minuscule, just a drop in the bucket... I've really been inspired by my peers... who serve alongside me and

the fact that the two of us, or the three of us or the twenty of us or the hundred of us can serve together. It's really energizing to me and gives me more hope and optimism that we can make a difference." — Vanderbilt University student

CITIZENS CAN MAKE A DIFFERENCE

"At one point, I think that I looked upon [community and social issues] and I dismissed them. But now since I've had the opportunity to work with students, see things — I'm encouraged to try to step in and make a difference."

— Clark Atlanta student

"It really came down to my privilege again. Of being able to do something for a few weeks and then pack up and go and that's not okay for me. And that's when the idea of actually doing service for life really came up. That I don't want to just go somewhere and drop it... we have a lot of power to change things and we can make a difference."

— University of Colorado student

"...I am more interested in working on the macro level. It's just that every issue and every policy has very personal implications..."

"I think there is a lot less perspective on their part [people who don't do service]. When you're in a class... it's all kinds of theory and ideas — it's really interesting but you don't feel it. And once you're in a situation where you're actually working with those people you're talking about in class — it makes it seem much more real and much more urgent to do something about..." — University of Washington student

Service-Learning Enhances Understanding of Issues and Subject Matter

When students discussed how service had enhanced their learning, the value of reflection to these students became clear. They found opportunities to share and discuss their experiences and to apply course concepts invaluable. All were not agreed upon the best form of reflection; as we shall see in Chapter 3, students had different orientations towards learning. But virtually all thought it was important to have multiple opportunities to reflect on what they were doing, and many were frustrated by the failure of faculty members to provide adequate feedback or opportunities for reflection.

In this section we will hear from students as they talked about how service and reflection enhanced their understanding of what they were studying. Students felt that they had a clearer grasp of the material being taught when service and learning were integrated.

They were able to understand theories and concepts when they saw examples in their service work. They often felt that their understanding was more three dimensional; they saw the complexities of issues that had seemed straightforward.

Part of this enhanced understanding may result from the enthusiasm for seeking answers to puzzles they confronted in the field; this motivational aspect of increased understanding was also addressed earlier in this chapter. Part of the understanding seems to come from the richer context for understanding material that is provided by experience in the community. And reflection forces students to observe and analyze what they observe and to articulate it and receive feedback from others.

The very act of writing or talking about one's experience can provoke insights that would otherwise never occur. And to reinforce the quotation at the beginning of this chapter, multiple opportunities to focus and reflect are critical to enhanced understanding. Students felt that they learned best when they were continuously challenged throughout the course of the term.

MAKING ABSTRACT CONCEPTS 'REAL'

"*It gives people more experience with what happens in the real world. You can go and you can look at things in class, you can read things in the library, but it's not really what happens. And you'll never know — People are more unpredictable than library research.*"

— University of Washington student

"*You can read theories in a classroom but you can't understand that until you hear a story and put a person's face to it and see their emotions.*"

— Vanderbilt University student

"*[I have learned to] respect experience. And, to picture things, to remember that every issue — I really am more interested in working on the political level – the macro level – it's just that every issue and every policy has very personal implications and hits the*

> **"...As we come out of school we're full of all these theories... But until we ... see them working in human lives... we're never going to really understand them..."**

particular homeless mother that I had pictured in my mind. It really just relates things to reality."

— University of Colorado student

"We learn these theories in school and ideas, but until we really apply them or see them in action, they're not real. And we come out of school, if we haven't done something like this – come out of school – not understanding. I think that as we come out of school we're full of all these theories and ideas and we've learned so much. But until we really apply them or see them working in human lives and in human beings — we're never going to really understand them. And we're going to come out of school and have a rude awakening. Cause there's the real world. I think it gives people a real perspective and I think a lot of people that I know that aren't naturally interested like I am in service, I think it would be a really important thing for them to do."

— University of Washington student

SEEING THE COMPLEXITY OF SOCIAL ISSUES

"I kept hearing things like — people are poor because they don't try or people are on welfare because they don't want to work. And I hear things like that. And it's definitely made me aware of how complex people's problems really are. That you can't answer it by saying — here's the answer and if you would just do what I say you should do, then your life would be better. It's just not like that."

— University of Washington student

"Service was enlightening, but at the same time it was more confusing because I learned that nothing is black and white and it's very gray. Does that make sense?"

— University of Colorado student

"*The bill doesn't make sense. It doesn't solve anything. It's similar to building prisons and throwing more people in prison. It doesn't solve why those people are out there. It doesn't solve why those people are committing violent crimes. What is it that makes them so angry? Why can't people get along without resorting to being violent? And it doesn't look at the problem of abuse — almost encourages abuse. Locking up kids is like — it doesn't solve anything... It is not one thing; that is what makes it so hard.*" — University of Washington student

USING THEORY FROM THE DISCIPLINES TO ORGANIZE EXPERIENCE

"*On one hand, the theory helps to organize what you see, sort of in society and what you're doing. It helps you organize that, but it doesn't really give you any prescriptive knowledge about what you're doing. It's more descriptive. [You understand things better] just because the personal experience is like a case example.*" — University of Washington student

"*[Describes how teacher uses characters from* Lives on the Boundary *and then asks students to find examples in their work in the field]. Then I'd jump in and say - I can see how the tracking does affect people... cause my homeless person was tracked at a very young age and put in a low track — never considered college because he wasn't in college classes where he could have been... So, right away we were seeing how tracking does affect people. Where if we just read it in a book that week, it wouldn't have mattered to us, we wouldn't have proof.*" — Bentley College student

> "**...[Our team] tries to talk at least once a week... One person might be in the first stage of a theory and another person might be in the third stage... we see how far the theory has gone with each person...**"

MULTIPLE REFLECTION TECHNIQUES AID UNDERSTANDING

"*All those things that we had to do for the service-learning. Each one successively helped me to pull together what I'd learned. As you're going along, you're not really seeing what you're learning every minute. But, when you have to pull it all together and really think about it, I think it helped me realize what had taken place.*"

— University of San Diego student

"*Well, in my opinion, I think that what's helpful for me is to have personal reflection and also group reflection. So, if I was going to structure a program, I would definitely incorporate ways for both of those. One thing that's been really helpful for me, and I didn't think it was helpful before I ever got into this program, was having small group discussions. And because I think there's something really important in having a voice and sharing your opinions and ideas and bouncing those off of other people.*"

— University of Colorado student

WRITING TO REMEMBER, CLARIFY AND ANALYZE EXPERIENCE

"*I've found answers to some questions just through writing what has happened.*"

"*After I write down my thoughts and everything, I can look back and find answers to questions that I thought were impossible to find. Like I've found answers to some questions just through writing what has happened.*"

— East Tennessee State University student

"*When you put something down on paper, it helps you straighten out your thoughts. Or helps me anyway. If I am confused about something or bungled up in my mind, if I can get it written down on paper and see exactly what experience I have had ... it straightens out my thinking.*"

— East Tennessee State University student

"*I went back and read it over again — nine weeks of writing every week... and I saw how my ideas changed and how my sensitivities changed. And I saw how these two little girls had changed.*"   — Clark Atlanta University student

"*[Journals are the most useful reflection] 'cause you write it the day you do your service... and you can go back and look and you can see progress — you can look back and say, how did this person progress? — what did I do to help them?*"

— Clark Atlanta University student

ORAL ASSIGNMENTS FACILITATE UNDERSTANDING

"*I think journals are pretty effective, but the problem with journals is that it's so self contained and you can't share your reflections with other people. 'Cause sometimes it takes like one word, where you're like, 'Wow' — from somebody else's mouth. That really helps you reflect more... I think it's really... sharing ideas within the group — verbalizing it — then everybody learns. Everybody gains.*"

— University of Colorado student

"*[Our team] tries to talk at least once or twice a week... and usually our experiences are different. So, one person might be in the first stage of a theory and another person might be in the third stage... so, it's like a show and tell. I say, 'Okay, I have this experience with my mentee' and then someone else will say, 'We did this' and 'This is my experience'. So we each can see how far the theory has gone with each person.*"

— University of San Diego student

Service-Learning Helps Students Apply Knowledge and Skills They Learn in One Setting to other Settings

The difference between passive classroom learning and experiential learning is sometimes described as the difference between 'knowing what' and 'knowing how'. It is the difference between inert knowledge and knowledge in use. The activities we have been discussing where students apply theories and concepts to the service experience in discussions, presentations and papers leads to a richer, more multidimensional *what*.

"*...I see people... making decisions... I don't think that they do service... I think they are missing the human element and how humans are affected by these decisions...*"

But students in service-learning also talk about the *how* of what they are learning. They see that service also contributes to the development of skills that allow them to apply what they are learning to new situations. These may be practical skills that will be useful to them on the job or in other service situations, or intellectual skills that help them make better judgments. Trying ideas out in practical settings is crucial to the transfer of learning and is part of what makes service-learning such a powerful educative experience.

SKILLS DEVELOPED IN ONE SERVICE ARENA MAY BE USED IN ANOTHER

"*When I went through RA training, we had to do a lot of written assignments about different things. And since I was involved with Student Hands and with rape education, I used those to do the written assignments. We talked about programs, like if you had to plan a program what would you do? And I used my service experiences to try to plan programs.*"

— Vanderbilt University student

"*People are so diverse and you can't know everything about everyone... For example, at the tutoring center, we realize that different students have different learning styles. And so part of our strategy is to have one-to-one tutoring so that the tutor can recognize... what the student's style is. You can't say to a student, 'If you only just — you would learn to read — or you would read better if you would only just learn to sound the words out.' Some students don't have the phonetic reading style... so, no matter how many times you try to pound into that kid, 'If you sound words out, you'll read better,' they're just never going to do it. I think that can be extrapolated to a larger social context. If you insist that people try to do things one way, it's not necessarily going to work for everyone. You have to have a varied approach.*"

— University of Washington student

"*I had never done anything like that. I was required to do that as a student leader; I facilitated for my class. I did it for the student leaders this semester. And it's good... I think I do a good job at it, but this was a different way of looking at it. It posed a challenge for myself and I know a lot of other people. So, It was a great reflection.*"

— University of San Diego student

APPLY SERVICE-LEARNING TO CITIZENSHIP DECISION-MAKING

"*When I read the newspaper and I see people making decisions, I always wonder if they really — I don't think that they do service, because if they did, I think that they would understand people at a more personal level... I think they are missing the human element and how humans are affected by these decisions that are made in society.*"

— University of Washington student

"*I think public officials need to talk and learn about the people that they affect when they make the decisions. So when they do welfare reform, they should go out and find out what it's like to live on welfare for a year. And maybe they'll decide, oh yes, it needs to be changed, but for many different reasons and maybe in a different way than they have before.*"

— Clark Atlanta University student

PRACTICING REAL WORLD SKILLS

"*We wrote a proposal — worked with a counselor in Boston. It didn't pass or anything and they keep working on it. But that was — our teacher was really excited about it too. 'Cause here we were taking real life stuff and trying to make a law... And all of us working on it had worked with homeless people for two years and we were really into it. And we understood that there are people out there that can't make those kinds of decisions. So we had to do research on it and we we found out that Chicago had tried it and New York had tried it. And New York actually took a person off [the street] and the person sued them and won. So that's an example of trying to do the right thing, but not getting the results.*

> **"...Instead of just doing a basic research project... we were actually trying to make something happen..."**

It's another thing that didn't work out in our favor, but it was something good, because here we are in a law class, but we're making it pertain to stuff that we're really interested in and we had a say and helped out a counselor a lot with our opinions and our experiences. Instead of just doing a basic research project on a topic in law, we were actually trying to make something happen." — Bentley College student

"We are working on increasing the individual donors and fund-raising [for a community service group needing to establish support after a 'seed grant' ran out] I talked to marketing professors here at school and other marketing students; I haven't gotten into marketing classes yet, but that's my major. So I'm talking to professors and getting their opinions on how to help and I'll be talking to other people at other shelters to find out what they do, so I can help my project... When I heard the chance to work at the food project and work with my major and learning more stuff about what I want to do later in life, I jumped at that chance... so when [an opportunity] comes up and I know that's going to help me in the future as well as help the people that I'm going to be working with - I think it's all the better."
— University of San Diego student

Service-Learning Coupled With Critical Reflection Helps Students Reframe the Way They Think about Complex Social Issues

Many students applied concepts to experience in order to understand them better, but some also engaged in a more fundamental exploration of their assumptions about society and knowing. Like the Grinch, they puzzled over contradictions between the way they thought the world was and what they were experiencing. By engaging in critical reflection they were sometimes able to see their society in a new way; they engaged in what Mesirow

(1990) calls *'transformative learning'*. This process occurred when they were confronted with powerful experiences and were challenged to question their assumptions.

CRITICAL REFLECTION AND SERVICE CHANGE THE WAY STUDENTS SEE THE WORLD

"[Before community service] I didn't really think a whole lot, like I thought of myself as a pretty smart person, but at the same time I hadn't developed the awareness of how interconnected the social structures are and how people are affected. I was really in a

tunnel vision of me and where I came from and I really hadn't broadened my horizons, so I think the first thing that I thought of — in the back of my head I had one of those old tapes that were like, 'Well, people are in their positions in life and everyone needs to be in this hierarchy,' and I don't know how to articulate it, not that people deserved what happened, but it happened for a reason. And when I got into INVST all those stereotypes were just destroyed... especially in the homeless experience."

"..When I got into [service-learning] all those stereotypes were just destroyed...."

— University of Colorado student

"I think I've become more politicized in my service. Growing up I didn't have the questions, the structural questions. I didn't see the inequities on a day to day basis that exist in our society that I see now or that I'm now connecting my service with... I see it much more as interconnected now. Before, social problems were — each problem needed to be attacked separately. I didn't see the correlation between, for example, racism and economic injustice... I grew up just not seeing the interconnection." — Vanderbilt University student

"I am not quite sure how to put this into words. I think that when I was in high school, when I was a lot younger and I wasn't really aware of the whys behind everything, I

thought of it as — here I am in this class and it was sort of an us and them sort of thing with people in the other class and kind of how my parents taught in a lot of respects the social structure — you belong here and they belong there. You can help them if you want to but you're not a part of their world and you stay separate. This sounds really condescending, but at the same time I thought — it was just sort of a thing that you can go help the people if you want to, but more like help them and now I think of it more

"...I think an important part of any [service] experience is that fact that you question continually..."

of working with... more of a thing where everyone is part of everyone else in a society and it's just as much your responsibility as everyone else's to do what you can... those connections - ...I've worked with people... and I've learned so much from everyone that I've met. With all these different people from all these different walks of life, I think I've taken something from and maybe given something to. And I see it more as a give and take sort of thing now than just sort of a give and help." — University of Colorado student

CONTINUITY COUPLED WITH CRITICAL REFLECTION LEADS TO TRANSFORMATION OF PERSPECTIVE

"I think an important part of any [service] experience is that fact that you question continually. And the best way that I can think of is for that to be an ongoing experience. It's easy when you go in once or twice, to go in the first time with preconceived ideas and look for information that affirms those ideas, even the second time... Only when you go through it and study a thing for — I want to say every week or every other week for a semester, will you really have your experiences challenged. But at the same time, if you don't reflect on it, it's easy to just keeping going there for the same assumptions. And operate on those. Only when you reflect and other people say, 'What about this?' or your professor writes in

your journal, 'What about this?' Then you go back and say, 'Well, she asked me about this, maybe I can look for this information.' So [it's important] to have this experience on an ongoing basis." — Vanderbilt University student

"...*That's what this reflection does, it really challenges people to do something that they're not used to doing. They see things in a different way...*"

"[Discussing a technique to force detailed analysis of service experience]. This was one of the better [reflection techniques] because it was a challenge. Anything that's a challenge, I think, makes you think things differently... It think everybody goes through their mindless... a mindless mentality and it's kind of the norm. When somebody's challenging you, I think they deviate from the norm, I think they get off track and it really makes them think of something differently. And I think that's what this reflection does, it really challenges people to do something that they're not used to doing. They see things in a different way and are able to analyze it or get something out of it that they normally wouldn't have." — University of San Diego student

POWERFUL PERSONAL EXPERIENCES BECOME THE FOCUS FOR REFRAMING

"...Something that really shocked me... was how I felt like people treated me preferentially because I was white — but I was given, I felt, pretty preferential treatment and other folks who were Latino told me that would happen... I was just surprised at how much that sort of racism is ingrained in things that I totally take for granted... I might be the only white person on the bus and that was a strange experience at first to be so in the minority like that... It made me forever feel more comfortable being in the minority. And it made me feel how so many people must feel in the dominant culture every day. I'd never thought about it when I was in a room full of people with only one person of color — how they

"

"...I might be the only white person on the bus... that was a strange experience at first ... It made me feel how so many people must feel in the dominant culture every day..."

"

must feel. Even though if the people in the room are welcoming them. It's still just odd to be the only one."

— University of Colorado student

"Well, I'll tell you a little personal story. One of my favorite students... was having the worst time trying to learn fractions. And I stayed after one day and we worked and we worked and he was saying things — I don't care, I don't want to learn. He finally picked it up. It was a Friday afternoon and he got it! His face lit up — like you can imagine and he said — 'It'll be so great. On Monday we'll do all the rest of this book and then I'll be caught up with my classmates when I go back to school. This is a whole new beginning for me.' He was like 15. And on Monday he didn't come to school. And I asked the site coordinator — 'what happened to [him]?' — Oh over the weekend, his sister stabbed him with a butcher knife and beat him over the head with a 2x4 — so, he's in the hospital, he's going to be okay, but - he's not coming to class for awhile. And I thought — why would he even care about school if your home environment is such that you can't — you have no ability to focus on school. So, I think what struck me most about that was the environments they were living in... I come from a very middle class upbringing. And the school system that I was in — we never confronted any of those problems... We had to evacuate [our service site] one day because we had word that there was going to be a gang drive by shooting... It was terrible conditions, but amazing — a part of America that I didn't even know existed at the time."   — University of Washington student

A Final Note

While all the students reported that they benefited from service, it was generally the students who were involved in formal, structured programs or in class-based service-learning who talked about the ways in which service improved their understanding, their ability to transfer what they had learned to new situations and the way they framed social issues. The critical component of effective service-learning was reflection with an **"R"**. The underlying themes for these students seemed to be that effective reflection involved the 4 C's. We can see in their stories the importance of **Continuous, Contextual, Challenging** and **Connected** reflection.

But there are a variety of ways in which this reflection might occur and different students emphasized different modes; some singled out discussion, or writing, or integration of reading and experience, while others stressed activities. Because different students respond to different forms of reflection, planning a service-learning curriculum should incorporate a variety of reflection activities. In Chapter 3, we will discuss how activities can be created for students with different learning styles, and in Chapter 4, we will share examples of specific activities that students found useful.

CHAPTER 2 REFERENCES

Giles, D.E., Jr & Eyler, J. "The Theoretical Roots of Service-Learning in John Dewey: Towards a Theory of Service-Learning." *Michigan Journal of Community Service-Learning Research*, 1(1), 1994.

Mezirow, J. & Associates. *Fostering Critical Reflection in Adulthood.* San Francisco: Jossey-Bass, 1990.

CHAPTER 3

DIFFERENT WAYS TO REFLECT AND LEARN

"And so, to hear the professor talk about a theory and then for her to say, 'Now here's a project – go do it.' And then, after the project's done, to say, 'Okay, what theory is applicable to this project?' The light bulb comes on. Okay, social penetration theory, that's what we're doing now. So, I understand it more by first having the assignment and then going out and doing it and then coming back and reflecting on it."

— University of San Diego student

This chapter focuses on the importance of recognizing distinct learning styles in order to select a variety of reflection activities. Before you read this chapter, consider the following statements and select the one that best describes your own preferred learning strategy:

1. I learn best about reflection by participating in a workshop on reflection in which participants have opportunities to reflect actively. I have completed the reflection activities that begin each chapter of this guide.

2. I learn best about reflection by observing colleagues as they use reflection activities with students or service-learning participants. I also tend to reflect on which reflection activities have worked best for me as a student or service-learning participant. I probably wrote notes in the margins of this manual to record reactions, questions and ideas I had in response to the text.

3. I learn best about reflection by maintaining a strong theoretical understanding of reflection and how it enhances learning. I immediately read Chapters 1 and 2 of this guide.

4. I learn best about reflection by experimenting with my own ideas in the classroom & in conjunction with service projects. Upon receiving this guide, I turned first to the activities in Chapter 4.

Although individuals use various methods to learn, they tend to have a learning style preference. If you identify most closely with Statement #1, you tend to learn by feeling. If Statement #2 most accurately represents your style, you tend to learn by watching and listening. If you chose Statement #3, you tend to learn by thinking and theorizing. Statement #4 connects with individuals who tend to learn by doing. As you read through this guide, reflect on the strengths and weaknesses of your particular learning style preference and work to identify strategies for enhancing your learning, utilizing different types of reflection activities.

USING INTERVIEW DATA TO STRUCTURE REFLECTION GUIDELINES:

Guidelines and examples discussed in this chapter as well as Chapter 4 were primarily formulated from interview data. Reflection activities used in service-learning can be categorized by the general headings of readings, written exercises, oral exercises, and projects and activities. Interview transcripts were coded for the following specific areas of reflection:

◆ *Activities:* simulations, movies, facilitating seminars, training sessions, etc.

◆ *Discussion:* structured, unstructured, analysis/application, etc.

◆ *Interaction:* community members, faculty, peers, staff, etc.

◆ *Journals:* group, reflective, unstructured, structured, oral, required, resource, observation, log, etc.

◆ *Oral Reflection:* feelings, listening, analysis/application, classroom presentations, etc.

◆ *Writing:* structured assignments, analysis/application, group, etc.

The most common forms of reflection the interviewees used in service-learning were discussion, interactions with others, and journals. Multiple factors contribute to the frequency or popularity of use of each particular type of reflection activity: faculty expertise and preference, academic credit vs. non-credit experience, resources needed, diverse learning styles of service-learning participants, and countless other factors.

LEARNING STYLES

Learning styles have a significant impact on the type of reflection activities in which participants engage. Ideally, service-learning faculty and coordinators should provide a variety of reflection activities and allow students some choice within that structure. Variety is important so that students "learn to learn" in different ways. David Kolb (1984) stresses the importance of challenging learners to engage in four different stages of learning — Concrete Experience, Reflective Observation, Abstract Conceptualization, and Active Experimentation — so that learning is a process. Kolb asserts that learning is most effective when the learner is fully engaged in a cycle of feeling (concrete experience), watching and listening (reflective observation), thinking (abstract conceptualization) and doing (active experimentation). This cycle allows action-reflection-action to occur.

Most learners have a tendency to learn using a combination of particular stages on the cycle. The end result is four learning styles. Homey and Mumford (Organizational Design and Development, Inc., 1989) have defined these four different learning styles or preferences: Activists, Reflectors, Theorists, and Pragmatists. It is useful to look at characteristics of each style to understand which type of reflection might be most useful to an individual service-learning participant.

THE EXPERIENTIAL LEARNING CYCLE

At the root of Dewey's phases of reflective thinking as well as of most major experiential learning theory lies a basic process. This process is simply "Action — Reflection — Action." The learner performs some action then reflects on the outcome of that action, making observations and developing explanations, and finally, the learner repeats the action phase, this time testing the observations or explanations developed during reflection. The result is a cyclical process, during which each action cycle is transformed as a result of plans and observations developed during the previous reflection cycle; and each reflection cycle expands the learner's world view based on observations from the previous action phase.

Kolb's cycle is based on this same foundational framework, and the "What? So What? Now What?" model grew out of Kolb's theories. The three are compiled below in the Experiential Learning Cycle, on which the remainder of this chapter is based.

Most individuals have a preferred stage of this learning cycle, and out of this preference we define an individual's preferred learning style, discussed in further detail on the next several pages.

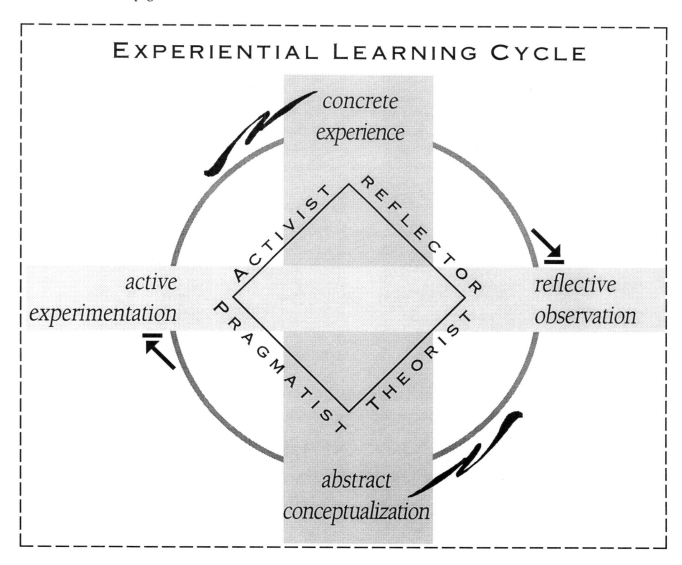

"...Once you discuss them in class, you get curious and you want to go out there and see for yourself...".

ACTIVIST:

■ Is oriented towards action

■ Acts first, considers the consequences later

■ Approaches life with "I'll try anything once" philosophy

■ Engages in activities fully and without bias

■ Focuses on the present

■ Tackles problems by brainstorming

■ Thrives on challenge; bored by implementation

■ Seeks attention, gregarious, people-oriented

■ Is primarily concerned with a need to adapt learning to own life situations to make more of what is learned

"Once you actually go out there, it's easier to help them. Once you discuss them in class, you get curious and you want to go out there and see for yourself."

— Clark Atlanta University student

"When you read a book and you kind of understand it, but until you experience it, it's harder to make a change. You read a book — oh, man, it really affected me — and then you put the book down. But you go and experience it and the book turns into a person, and then that person affect you. And it's harder to put a person and put that person aside and say, 'Oh, that didn't really happen.' Or, 'Okay, I understand now, but I'm just going to go on the way I've always lived.'" — University of Colorado student

"We had to make a presentation to the class and it was on about anything, if I remember correctly. The presentation was a free for all. You could discuss, share with a class about a change in the atmosphere or something you observed or whatever. And what I ended up doing, is I invented a learning game. And I made a mock-up of it and presented to the class. It was fun, it was scary. But it was also, for me, it was exciting to do something that really stretched me. And it was innovative."

— University of Washington student

REFLECTOR:

- Ponders experiences and observes

- Seeks data and considers thoroughly

- Postpones decision-making until data is available

- Watches and listens before offering own opinions

- Acts within a larger framework and after considering all angles

- Is primarily concerned with creating personal meaning out of experience

"...I internalized them and I think about them to myself. I don't necessarily verbalize to people..."

"I'm more of an observer. So, if I do something, I'm more of a person who can just sit there and watch people. And so when I sit back and I look at the Senior Olympics or the recreation projects that we have for the kids for Halloween, to me to sit there and just watch the kids works best."

— University of San Diego student

"I internalized them and I think about them to myself. I don't necessarily verbalize to people. That may be why I'm having a little difficulty... But when things affect me personally is when I take them to heart. The kid giving me a kiss on the cheek was — wow, look how happy he is from something I've done. And I think I just really internalize things, and I think about them a lot to myself and it makes me more motivated to do something." — University of San Diego student

"I had to come back and address the class on what I observed, the surroundings and then what they told me. How they perceived it. How I perceived it. If that was different and why. Each student took a different agency, so we were in charge of coming back and telling them all about that agency or at least what we could find out."

— East Tennessee State University student

Structuring Reflection ◆ Chapter 3

❖ R e f l e c t i o n   G u i d e   ◆   P a g e   5 1 ❖

"...Take a problem and break it down, step by step by step and get to the root structures of why..."

THEORIST:

- Approaches problems using vertical, step-by-step approach
- Pulls together disparate facts into cogent theories
- Seeks perfection
- Prizes rationality and logic
- Dislikes flippancy and uninformed decision-making

"Well, what helped me to reflect upon it was in my clinical lab course, which basically teaches what you need to know - it's entitled, Learning to Teach. It teaches you what to know as a teacher. We were discussing punishing students and I brought that incident up to my instructor and we discussed it for an entire class period, the whole class included and we just basically came to the agreement that there is a need for discipline in the schools, but not at the expense of breaking the self esteem or damaging the child physically. Those were the conclusions we came to." —Clark Atlanta student

"Last spring in our Solving Community Problems course, we did some very tedious diagnostic analysis of take a problem and break it down, step by step by step and get to the root structures of why — What's supporting the problem? Who are your adversaries? Which ways are we not seeing? And the whole idea of reframing — How can we reframe our problem? What are some creative solutions to this problem? Those are the most helpful for me." — University of Colorado student

"Another great thing we do in the English class is we took literacy — not just with the homeless people, but with any aspect of it. We looked at grade school tracking with literacy and how people became illiterate during tracking. I looked at prisoners. So, here I was taking prisoners - if they are illiterate, are they more apt to commit crime. So, I was taking what I learned through literacy to crime." — Bentley College student

PRAGMATIST:

- Tries and tests ideas, theories and techniques
- Acts quickly and confidently to implement ideas
- Dislikes ruminating and open-ended discussions
- Displays practical problem-solving and decision-making skills
- Sees problems as opportunities

"...That was a challenge to be able to not just see someone else's ideas through, but to create my own ideas about how to do things...".

"What we basically do is we take a particular problem and we relate it to information from the text. For example, the Wednesday past, we talked about class management. There's a lady in the class that seemed to be having a problem with a student that constantly wanted to disrupt the class. So, what we did was we looked at the chapter in our text which dealt with classroom management and we figured out that maybe if she was to give that student more work, maybe then that problem would subside. Or maybe if she pulled that student aside and worked with him individually again, that could eradicate that problem. So, we constantly take real life situations and apply it to what's in the book so that we can intermingle the two and come up with solid conclusions for problems that are relevant." — Clark Atlanta University student

"I felt it would be a new opportunity to approach the issues that I'd been working with and I was eager to take on leadership positions... [It was important] because I wanted to implement some of my own ideas about how we could handle or get other students involved or — we were writing our own programs. So, to me, that was a challenge to be able to not just see someone else's ideas through, but to create my own ideas about how to do things." — University of San Diego student

SELECTING AND USING REFLECTION ACTIVITIES

The key to selecting reflection activities is to look critically at the kinds of ideas, exercises and experiences that connect with each individual in the group. Naturally, any group will contain a spattering of Theorists, Pragmatists, Reflectors and Activists; and meeting the needs of all learning style preferences at different times should be a priority.

Certain types of activities fit naturally into learning style preference categories. In order to ease the process of selecting reflection activities for any project or course, we have categorized the activities in this guide according to the four basic types consistently mentioned by student interviewees: Reading, Writing, Doing and Telling. Each method has its own inherent strengths and weaknesses and tends to meet the needs of certain learning styles better than others. The next few pages should offer some guidance for recognizing and managing the strengths and weaknesses of various reflection methods so as to connect with the broad range of learning styles that make up your group. Use this information to guide your selection of reflection activities.

DIFFICULTY USING CERTAIN STYLES

The flip side to the strengths of each learning style or type of reflector is that each individual may struggle with learning methods that do not suit his or her own natural learning style.

"We have to keep a journal. It's supposed to be connected to the course material, but I have no idea how I'm supposed to do that. Because most of our course material has been on affirmative action and I'm not sure how to tie it in with... I'm having a tough time..."

— University of San Diego student

It is critical that the selection of reflection activities for a given project or course contain something for everyone, or individuals with certain learning styles may disengage from the process, robbing the group of the wisdom and balance that those learning styles would offer. Whenever possible, a facilitator may offer a choice of reflection activities to allow each individual to select a method that connects with his or her own learning preferences.

When this is impossible or undesirable, faculty and coordinators need to be prepared to spend additional time with students who have difficulty with a particular type of reflection. Be aware of the learning styles operating within your group, and be purposeful about seeking out individuals that you suspect may need assistance with certain segments of the reflection process.

Although each student has a naturally preferred learning style, the depth of the learning process can also be strengthened by working to expand students' capacity to engage in a variety of reflection methods. Self-awareness of preferred learning styles is the first step in broadening ways to learn. Most students can intuit their particular learning style by reading the descriptions in this chapter, but the Learning Style Inventory (LSI) from McBer and Co. (see appendix for more information) is a more directed assessment of learning style preferences.

If students recognize the strengths and weaknesses of their own learning tendencies, and feel that the needs of their learning styles are met regularly, they will also be able to work on other methods of learning without feeling that they are missing out on the reflection itself while struggling with uncomfortable learning methods. For example, if an individual tends to be a *'reflector'* when learning, journals will be an important tool to encourage reflection and learning. On the other hand, this individual should also engage in more active types of reflection such as simulations, role plays, conferences, or presentations in order to develop other learning styles.

AN EXTRA NOTE

◆

In addition to being useful tools to guide individual learning, learning style preferences can be used to help individuals understand their strengths and weaknesses in a team settting.

◆

Service project coordinators can also use learning style preferences to construct diverse teams of service-learning participants.

READING: *Literature and Written Materials*

'*Theorists,*' who learn best through abstract conceptualization, tend to read literature and materials as a learning strategy. These readings usually provide rational and logical models and theories which help students make sense of their experience.

- ◆ Case Studies

- ◆ Books about social issues

- ◆ Government documents

- ◆ Professional journals

- ◆ Classic literature

- ◆ Refer to Resources List at the end of Chapter 4 for specific suggestions.

Strengths

■ Increases understanding of a particular issue.

■ Allows students to read various perspectives on an issue

■ Helps students prepare for service

■ Activity is self-paced and can be done almost anywhere.

Guidelines

1. Use a variety of sources.

2. If possible, have students create their own reading lists.

3. Always debrief readings orally or in writing.

4. Draw clear links between the reading and the service experience.

Weaknesses

■ Materials can become quickly outdated.

■ Professional journals can be difficult to read and understand.

■ Students may have difficulty applying their readings to their experience.

■ Some students avoid lengthy reading.

WRITING: *Written Exercises*

'Theorists' and *'Reflectors'* tend to use writing as a way to reflect on experiences and integrate experiences with models and theories. *'Pragmatists'* will use writing to propose practical ideas or projects which evolved out of learning.

- Journals and logs
- Reflection essays
- Self-evaluation essays
- Portfolios
- Analysis papers
- Case studies
- Grant proposals
- Press releases
- Drafting legislation
- Letters to other students/clients/self/politicians
- Published articles (newspapers, newsletters, journals)
- Volunteer/Agency training manuals

Strengths

■ Students practice writing skills.

■ Students are forced to structure thoughts and present them in an articulate way.

■ Provides permanent records which students can revisit at future times.

■ May provide real service by producing something that community groups need.

Guidelines

1. Assign a combination of structured analytical writing and unstructured narrative writing.

2. Provide extensive feedback on content and style.

3. Allow students to reflect on feedback they receive.

4. Ensure confidentiality of journals.

5. Consider assigning some writing which will not be evaluated for a grade.

6. Design projects to produce actual products community groups can use.

Weaknesses

■ Is not interactive.

■ Assignments tend to be time-consuming.

■ Requires extensive feedback.

■ Some students stated that they "wrote what the professor wanted to hear" rather than what they honestly thought.

DOING: *Projects and Activities*

'Activists' tend to learn by involving themselves actively in a particular project or exercise. Projects use the strengths of all learning styles.

- Simulations

- Conducting interviews

- Art journal

- Role playing

- Collecting photos, creating slide presentations

- Watching movies/videos

- Presentations involving dance, music, or theatrics

- Planning public relations events for the agency

- Analyzing or creating agency budgets

- Program development

Strengths

- Is conducive to group projects.

- Engages multiple skills and learning styles.

- Allows students to be self-directed.

- Often involves "real work" for community group, rather than academic exercise.

Guidelines

1. Provide or have students establish goals for each activity.

2. Engage students in reflection throughout the various stages of the activity.

3. Encourage use of various learning strategies and styles.

4. Provide constructive feedback.

5. Debrief each activity.

6. Refer students to community experts for technical assistance on projects.

Weaknesses

- Generally requires extensive monitoring and feedback.

- Requires thorough debriefing if critical reflection is to occur.

- Weakens control over outcome.

- Time frame must be monitored closely.

TELLING: *Oral Exercises*

'*Activists*' tend to reflect and learn through speaking and oral presentations in order to effect change and impact a particular group of people.

- Focus groups

- Informal discussions

- Formal class discussions

- Presentations

- Talking to other students

- Recruiting other volunteers

- Teaching a class

- Cooperative learning

- Story telling

- Individual conferences with faculty or project sponsor

- Legislative testimony

Strengths

■ Allows for practice of oral presentation skills.

■ Provides opportunity for dialogue.

■ Allows for expression with nonverbal behavior as well.

■ May challenge students' observations and assumptions.

Guidelines

1. Provide constructive feedback.

2. Videotape formal presentations when possible for feedback.

3. Establish a climate where each member of a group is expected to participate.

4. Provide clear instructions for group processes [Cooperative Learning, Nominal Group Technique, etc.]

Weaknesses

■ Some students have difficulty with public speaking.

■ No permanent record is created, unless videotaped.

■ Facilitator needs conflict management skills.

A FEW FINAL WORDS

You will find that the Reflection Activity Matrix on Page 65 links these four learning methods — Reading, Writing, Doing, and Telling — to the reflection outcomes detailed in Chapter 2: Personal Development, Connecting to Others, Citizenship Development, Understanding, Application, and Reframing. The matrix will allow you to select specific activies that combine the methods of Doing, for example, with the outcomes of Self-Development and Understanding.

CHAPTER 3 REFERENCES

Homey, P. & Mumford, A. *Learning Styles Questionnnaire*. Organization Design and Development, Inc. Pennsylvania: King of Prussia, 1989.

Kolb, D.A. *Experiential Learning: Experience as the Source of Learning and Development*. Englewood Cliffs, New Jersey: Prentice-Hall, 1984

CHAPTER 4
PUTTING REFLECTION INTO ACTION

"*[The most effective reflection] is what we are doing now for this communication theory course. It is by going out, experiencing and then coming back and writing about it and talking about it within your group. And then talk about it in front of the classroom. Because then, it like pounds it into your head... Okay, I can talk about it; I can write about it; I know it inside and out. So that's the most positive reflection I think.*"

— University of San Diego Student

This chapter provides concrete examples of how to create an experiential learning curriculum for service-learning programs and courses using reflection activities. Based on our interviews, we were able to identify the types of reflection students find most useful: Reading, Writing, Doing, and Telling. Chapter 3 discusses the importance of honoring students' learning style preferences and encouraging use of a variety of learning activities; in order to do this effectively, it is crucial to recognize that certain types of activities are better suited to achieving certain outcomes.

The matrix on page 65 catalogues several outcomes of service-learning and reflection, as identified by students. These outcomes are described in Chapter 2 and are similar to those discussed by Silcox (1993) in his very useful book, *A How-To Guide to Reflection: Adding Cognitive Learning to Community Service Programs.* Although each outcome can be achieved through a variety of activities, some may be more easily attained using particular types of learning. For example, citizenship development is enhanced when students are called on to serve as 'experts,' and personal development is enhanced by use of reflective journals. Both the matrix on Page 65 and Silcox's matrix can be

Building on what you have learned about reflection in previous chapters, create four different reflection activities for a topic you will use in class. Most service-learning experiences focus on a particular social problem (e.g. homelessness, environmental waste, child abuse, AIDS, teenage pregnancy).

Select a particular social problem and design a series of learning experiences which include each of the following activities: reading, writing, doing, telling. As you create these activities, keep in mind how learning style preferences impact learning, and use the 4 C's (Continuous, Connected, Challenging, Contextualized) to guide your design.

useful in designing a curriculum and in evaluating learning outcomes. The inherent multiplicity of outcomes for service-learning naturally allows a curriculum to contain diverse reflection activities.

The general pattern which emerged from the interviews, regardless of activity type, confirms that the more students are challenged to think critically and connect theory to practice, the more likely they are to "reframe" their learning. Informal discussions were cited as extremely important in encouraging self development and helping students connect to others. Students felt their understanding of social issues was deepened when they were asked to apply what they were learning to the field and when they were called upon to present material or instruct others. Critical reflection or "reframing" is best achieved through structured oral or written reflection, which challenges their assumptions. Learning can best be achieved by using the four C's discussed in Chapter 1 to design a curriculum. It is important to structure reflection within a particular **context,** push and **challenge** students to reframe they way they think, make reflection **continuous,** throughout a course and throughout the college career, and use reflection to **connect** theory to practice.

HOW TO USE THIS CHAPTER

Your use of Chapter 4 will depend on your own teaching and learning style as well as your immediate curricular needs:

1. *If you are looking for concrete exercises to adapt to your current class or service-learning project...*

...you can select from individual activities in the Reflection Activity Matrix on Page 65. The Reflection Activity matrix is designed to help you find activities according to outcome and type. Four sections of reflection activities follow: Reading, Writing, Doing and Telling, each with its own "Table of Contents" to clarify page numbers once again. The icons should help you easily distinguish among Reading, Writing, Doing and Telling methods and types of activities. Some of the activities have multiple icons as they are appropriate for and easily adapted to different types of learning. For example, some of the questions in the writing exercises can effectively be used for oral discussions.

READING   WRITING

DOING   TELLING

2. *If you are creating a new service-learning curriculum...*

...you might want to begin this process by reviewing the case study at the end of this chapter. The case study is an example of how to sequence activities in the chapter so that reflection is appropriately **contextualized, challenging, continuous,** and **connects** theory to practice.

3. *If you have defined specific outcomes for which you need an activity...*

...you can locate activities in the matrix that are designed to achieve these outcomes and use them as models. Student quotations and suggested variations for activities should help you to build on the examples provided here, creating similar activities that will meet the needs of your particular learning agenda.

Reflection Activity Matrix

	READING	WRITING	DOING	TELLING
PERSONAL DEVELOPMENT	❖The Role of Service [p.68]	❖Letters Home [p.76] ❖Group Journal [p.77] ❖Personal Journals [p.78] ❖Portfolio [p.82]	❖Student Facilitation [p.102] ❖Artistic Reflection [p.105]	❖Encouraging Informal Discussion [p.128] ❖Mentoring [p.130] ❖Reflective Interview [p.131]
CONNECTING TO OTHERS	❖The Role of Service [p.68]	❖Letters Home [p.76] ❖Group Journal [p.77]	❖Student Facilitation [p.102] ❖Artistic Reflection [p.105] ❖Oral Histories [p.108]	❖Encouraging Informal Discussion [p.128] ❖Mixed Discussion Groups [p.133] ❖Reflecting *with* the Community [p.135]
CITIZENSHIP DEVELOPMENT	❖The Role of Service [p.68]	❖Letters Home [p.76] ❖Letters & Memos [p.85]	❖Artistic Reflection [p.105] ❖Oral Histories [p.108] ❖Policy Action [p.110] ❖Health Fairs [p.113]	❖Reflecting *with* the Community [p.135]
UNDERSTANDING	❖Using Case Studies to Prepare for Service [p.70]	❖Group Journal [p.77] ❖Personal Journals [p.78] ❖Portfolio [p.82] ❖Letters & Memos [p.85] ❖Integrative Papers [p.88] ❖Organizational Analysis [p.91] ❖Critical Questions [p.95] ❖Applying Kolb's Model [p.97]	❖Student Facilitation [p.102] ❖Oral Histories [p.108] ❖Service-Learning Theater [p.114] ❖Using Films & Videos [p.116] ❖Field Data Gathering [p.118]	❖Informal Discussion [p.128] ❖Mixed Discussion Groups [p.133] ❖Mentoring [p.130] ❖"Service is Like..." [p.138] ❖Three Questions [p.139] ❖Large Group Discussion [p.141] ❖Reading Journals Aloud [p.144] ❖Focus Groups for Reflection & Evaluation [p.146] ❖Oral Presentations [p.148]
APPLICATION	❖Using Case Studies to Prepare for Service [p.70]	❖Portfolio [p.82] ❖Letters & Memos [p.85 ❖Integrative Papers [p.88] ❖Organizational Analysis [p.91] ❖Applying Kolb's Model [p.97]]	❖Policy Action [p.110] ❖Health Fairs [p.113] ❖Student Facilitation [p.101] ❖Service-Learning Theater [p.114]	❖Reflective Interviews [p.131] ❖Three Questions [p.139] ❖Reading Journals Aloud [p.144] ❖Oral Presentations [p.148]
REFRAMING	❖Point/Counterpoint [p.72]	❖Integrative Papers [p.88] ❖Organizational Analysis [p.91] ❖Critical Questions [p.95]	❖Policy Action [p.110] ❖Tapped into Citizenship — a Simulation [p.119] ❖World Hunger Simulation [p.122] ❖"The Watch" - Critical Reflection [p.124]	❖Reflective Interviews [p.131] ❖Reflecting *with* the Community [p.135] ❖Reflecting on Cultural Identity [p.150]

READING

The Role of Service

One goal of service-learning involvement is to push students to develop a sense of the importance of service and to develop their skillfulness as community volunteers. As students become more experienced they may see service in a more complex way and take on more responsible roles. Explicit models of service or stories about the impact of service can provide a platform for exploring these issues.

PURPOSE:

Personal Development

◆

Connecting to Others

◆

Citizenship Development

"*I think we all moved along the continuum... from charity to justice. I read about that.' Or from the continuum of volunteering to social action. Or the continuum could just be from doing service to being thoughtful about service.*"

— Vanderbilt University student

PREPARATION

Students read an article or book that describes various stages or types of community service involvement, the socialization of volunteers, or the role of service in effecting social change. The reading is then used as an 'anchor' piece for reflection and analysis during the course of the service-learning.

REFLECTION

The reflective component of this activity can take various forms. The reading can serve as a foundation for large or small group discussion, personal journaling, or more formal papers. In their initial reflections on their service they might:

◆ Compare their own experiences with those they have read during preparation.

◆ Discuss difficulties they are having in their site and reflect on how the individuals they have read about would handle similar problems.

◆ Create models that capture stages of experience based on their own experiences and those of volunteers with whom they have worked.

◆ Evaluate their own 'stage' of involvement in community service. Towards the end of the service experience, reflection might move from current experience to future experience and more explicit concerns with the role of service in one's life.

◆ Identify goals for future levels and types of involvement.

◆ Create definitions of community service — and what it means in their lives now.

"...The essays do in a way relate back to your specific community service. And it's usually about people helping people or indirectly — there is one that we just read, it was about a woman — it was called Chatterbox — all she did was talk and she drove her husband away, she drove her son away and then she went to an old age home and she talked to them — and sure enough she went there weekly and her problem was solved. So, not only was she helping other people, but she cured herself too. I think in a way, in community service — like I'm helping these girls out — but also, they're teaching me — about how it is to be on the other side and how it is not to have everything that I have."

— Bentley College student

SAMPLE READINGS

There are a number of books and articles about service that could serve to anchor students' reflections about the role of service and their own development as citizens.

Bellah, R. *Habits of the Heart: Individualism and Commitment in American Life.* Berkeley: University of California Press, 1985

Colby, A. *Some Do Care: Contemporary Lives of Moral Commitment.* New York: Free Press, 1992

Coles, R. *The Call of Service: A Witness to Idealism.* Boston: Houghton Mifflin Co., 1993

Covey, S. *The Seven Habits of Highly Effective People: Restoring the Character Ethic.* New York: Simon & Schuster, 1989

Delve, D., Mintz, S.D., & Stewart, G.M., Eds. *Community Service as Values Education.* San Francisco: Jossey-Bass, 1990

Peavey, F. *Heart Politics.* Philadelphia: New Society Publishers, 1986

SOURCE
Students from several schools.

Using Case Studies to Prepare for Service

Case studies or stories of service help broaden student experience and also serve as a model to help students focus on what to look for when they begin their community service.

PURPOSE:

♦

Understanding

♦

Application

"*I didn't know places like that existed. Well, I did, right before I went on the trip, because we were asked to read the book* Rachel and Her Children, *and that just kind of tore away the band-aid that I thought was on me, the ignorance and complacency. So, I was like this sponge just soaking it up during that experience.*"

— University of Colorado student

OVERVIEW

Students read case studies related to their area of service. Case studies are available in the form of books and other published materials (see suggestions on facing page), can be "collected" by compiling articles from local newspapers and media, and are recyclable: case studies created or compiled by former students make excellent preparatory reading material for future students. The case material then may be used in a variety of ways:

♦ Use before service to help students think about what to expect and to help them plan questions to pursue during their service.

♦ Ask students to compare the events of the case to the situations they experience during service.

♦ Students develop their own case studies and share them with classmates.

"It was almost like he would bring up a situation that a character in the book was dealing with. And then he'd say, 'Can you see how this would relate to someone you guys are working with?' — we would be doing our own investigating. I'd be asking the person I was tutoring, 'What was grade school like for you?' Then, I'd jump in or someone would

jump in and say, 'I can see how the tracking does affect people — if we're talking how it affects kids at a young age, cause my homeless person was tracked at a very young age and put in a track — never considered college because he wasn't in college prep classes where he could have been — and never went to college.' So right away, we are seeing how tracking does affect people. Where if we just read it in a book that week, it wouldn't have mattered to us; we wouldn't have proof. Now, if you actually hear it from someone, it makes a big difference from just reading it."

— University of Washington student

❖

CASE STUDY RESOURCES TO USE

Albert, G. *Service-Learning Reader: Reflections and Perspectives on Service.* Raleigh, NC: National Society for Experimental Education, 1995

Kozol, J. *Rachel and Her Children: Homeless Families in America.* New York: Crown Publishers, 1988.

Peavey, F. *Heart Politics.* Philadelphia: New Society Publishers, 1986

Rose, M. *Lives on the Boundary: the Struggles and Achievements of America's Underprepared.* New York: Free Press, 1989

Verghese, A. *My Own Country: a Doctor's Story of a Town and its People in the Age of AIDS.* New York: Simon & Schuster, 1994.

SOURCE
Students from several schools.

Point: Counterpoint

Many students find it difficult to question their assumptions and engage in critical reflection. By presenting contrasting perspectives on the same issue, the process can be made explicit.

"*Well, a lot of the things we've read this year have definitely — like we've even read stuff on reframing, being able to look at situations and to interpret them differently than your consciousness takes them in to be. And that's part of ingesting information that is so different — like we read a lot of different feminist perspectives — books that definitely bring in a whole lot of different changes in the way you are thinking.*"

— University of Colorado student

PURPOSE:

•

Reframing

PROCESS

STEP 1

Students are asked to read articles with conflicting positions or perspectives on issues related to their field service.

STEP 2

Contrasting assumptions that underlie these views are then explored. Students are asked to discuss their related experiences in the field:

♦   What have you seen that is consistent [or inconsistent] with the assumptions and views presented?

♦   How would the authors of the various articles see and interpret the field experiences you are having?

♦   What perspective do the people you are working with seem to have on these issues? Why? How do you know that?

♦   What do you think? How is that supported by your experience in the community?

♦   Has your perspective changed during your community service?

"*Cause each time — each new assignment, well, this is the way I think — and then another assignment is assigned and it's like... maybe it should be this way. But, usually within each assignment there's three readings that we have to reflect on — so, there actually has been a good amount of reading that we've had to reflect on.*"

— Bentley College student

SAMPLE TOPICS MENTIONED BY STUDENTS:

◆ Pros and cons of tracking students in school

◆ Desirability of day care for children as compared with mothers staying with the children

◆ Pros and cons of HIV testing and informing parents of newborns of their HIV status.

◆ Desirability of more prison and punishment contrasted with other approaches to criminal behavior.

◆ Social justice critiques by feminists and members of ethnic minorities.

"*A lot of our readings were male/female roles. There would be an argument for and an argument against something. Like working parents are good for their kids and an article, working parents are bad for the kids, there should be somebody staying at home. Those were interesting. I thought it was frustrating, that the titles had working parents and the article was about how the mom worked. She was wrong or she was right. Why is it always assumed that the woman should or shouldn't be working? And a lot of those reasons were about unforseen parenthood. And that was insightful for me on the girls [that I was working with], who were about to be single parents.*"

— University of San Diego student

SOURCE
Students from University of San Diego, Bentley College, University of Colorado and University of Washington.

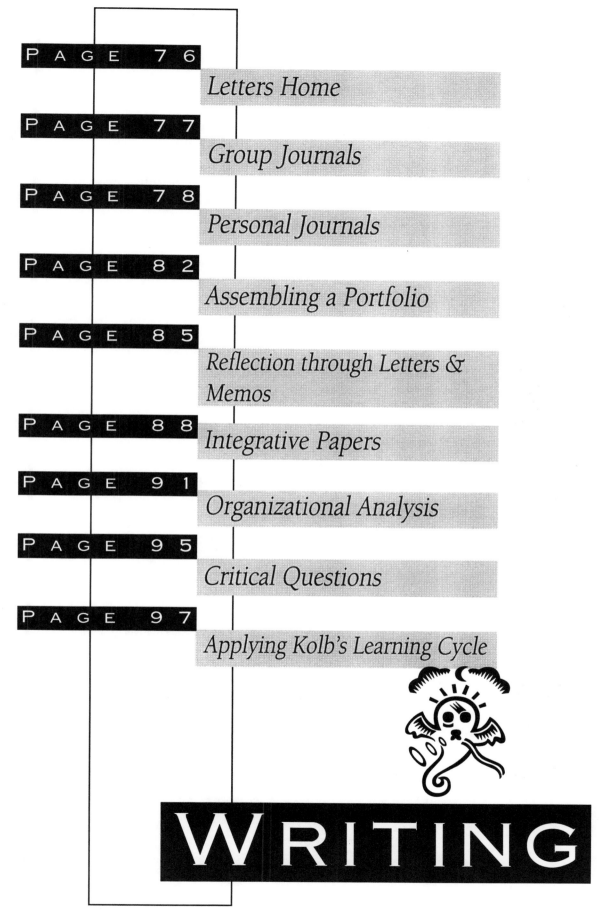

WRITING

Letters Home

Family and friends are often concerned when students choose service that takes them into a community very different from their own; this fear is heightened for intensive experiences like alternative breaks or service internships where students will live and work in the community. When the student team develops a letter to parents, spouses and other family members, detailing their plans and their reasons for involvement, it helps them reflect on their own motivation as well as reassure their families.

PROCESS

Students list the concerns that have been expressed. Students discuss how best to respond to each concern as well as a strategy for the design of the letter.

For example, a group of 15 students in a policy class planning an ASB week working with AIDS projects in a distant city decided to explain:

- how the project enhanced their classroom learning

- why service was important to them

- the specific activities they would be involved in

- the specific travel and housing arrangements

- the training they were receiving before the trip

The letter is then drafted by student volunteers and critiqued by the group. The final version is sent by the students to their friends and relatives.

At the completion of the project, a similar letter may be drafted which focuses on what the students felt they achieved in their service. The two letters can also serve as a focus for group discussion of how their attitudes and understandings have changed with their service.

PURPOSE:

Personal Development

◆

Connecting to Others

◆

Application

SOURCE
Vanderbilt ASB/Policy Class

Group Journals

Students in intensive service experiences like Alternative Spring Break may feel overwhelmed; the demands of the service may make structured reflection difficult to conduct. Group journals have the value of encouraging students to put their thoughts and perceptions in writing while not placing pressure on individuals. They also promote thoughtful interaction.

PROCESS

◆   Provide a notebook which is kept in an accessible place where students congregate after their service.

◆   Students are invited to contribute to the group journal. They may share their insights or respond to experiences described by other participants. It is particularly useful as a record of changing perceptions and experiences over the course of the service.

◆   At the end of the service assignment, copies of the journal can be made and distributed to all participants.

VARIATIONS

◆   Select one person to record each day's events to ensure that a continuous record is kept. Then encourage other individuals to add commentary, art, even shared jokes from the events.

◆   Use a group journal in a classroom setting. Assign each student a page, and ask for contributions reflecting the power of their service experiences. Or ask each student to create a case study of his or her organization or experience; then use the resulting collection as reading material for another reflection activity [See Using Case Studies for Prepare for Service, Page 70].

"We just kept the journal in our room and people would write, sometimes long essays and sometimes just quick notes on what they were thinking... and sometimes people would sort of dialogue, but through the journal . . and when we were back home, we copied it and everyone had their own copy of the group journal."

— Vanderbilt University student

PURPOSE:

Personal Development
◆
Connecting to Others
◆
Understanding

SOURCE
Vanderbilt and Bentley students

Personal Journals

Student interviewees tended to have a love-hate relationship with journaling. Written reflection, especially frequent writing, was widely viewed as the most important technique for learning, yet many students found it difficult to do.

" I don't like to keep a journal... but the assignment that really helped me get things clear in my mind was the journal keeping... taking the issues and turning them around and making them personal to the experiences we were having in our service project - it was taking the academic and making it personal." — University of Colorado student

A particular benefit of journaling is that it creates a written record of progress over the course of a term; the document can become a useful focus for reflection on personal growth and on changing perceptions.

PURPOSE:

Personal Development

◆

Understanding

"For me, I think, it's good for me to write things down. Like taking the journals. It was great because it was a form of expression and memory... I'll forget what I was experiencing and when I was writing the paper, it was interesting to go back and recall the trouble I had in the very beginning and then my impression later and how it had changed."

— Clark Atlanta student

PROCESS

There are a variety of ways to use journals, with varying degrees of structure They may be largely open ended and personal or they may be an integral part of the curriculum. The other activities in this chapter can easily be converted into or followed by a journaling assignment — to add an individualized component to a shared group reflection experience, for example, or to create case studies and other materials that can later be used as part of a reading activity. When used as part of a class, students were clear that frequent feedback was critical to their success.

Structured Journals

STANDARD QUESTIONS

Some students were asked to respond to a standard set of questions with each journal entry. This technique builds continuity and familiarity with the reflective process.

- What happened today?
- What did you do?
- What were the effects of what you did?
- How do you feel about that?
- How does what you are observing at your placement relate to what we are doing in class?

APPLIED THEORIES

Many students were asked to apply specific theories to what they were observing in their service setting. The journal became the tool for linking theory with practice.

Examples of theories used in this assignment:

- Theories of conflict
- Social penetration
- Communication
- Gender
- Leadership
- Learning
- Organizational behavior.

VARIED QUESTIONS

Others were given different tasks and questions to include in their journals which changed as the semester progressed. Initially they might be asked:

- What are your first impressions?
- How do you feel about the people you are working with?
- What is different than you expected?

Later questions might include:

- What have you been able to accomplish in your service?
- What are the biggest problems faced by your organization in meeting the needs of the people served?

GUIDELINES FOR STUCTURED JOURNALS:

Feedback

Instructor responds to or uses student journals in further assignments or discussion — proves that journaling is not "busy work".

◆

Structure

Instructor provides journal prompts related to each experience to guide reflective process.

◆

Context

Instructor finds creative ways to encourage reflection appropriate to the nature of the program, and through both personal and group journals.

◆

Sensitivity to Learning Styles

Instructor provides support for students who may be less comfortable with writing — may use journaling as a base for role plays, group discussion and other reflection activities.

◆

Goal Match

Instructor encourages structure & use of journal to match the goals of the service-learning experience — some may be focused on affective dimensions of the experience; others serve as a resource base and analytical tool.

CRITICAL INCIDENTS

Critical incidents may also be included in journals and serve as the basis for class discussion or other activities. A form used by one program to gather critical incident material is included in the Doing section, as part of Service-Learning Theater [See page 114] and can be adapted as a journal instruction.

ROLE TAKING

Some students were asked to write about their service experience from different perspectives. For example, they might do a journal entry from the perspective of the people receiving service or another from the perspective of an administrator at the site.

"Students have been asked to write about their service experience from a different perspective... write a journal from someone who received the benefits of the service... or from a third disinterested party who just happened to observe... or someone who is an administrator in a school where you tutor..."   — Vanderbilt University student

Free Form Journals

Some programs ask students to keep journals, but allow them to structure them as they like. The effectiveness of the class in combining service and learning may be reflected in the quality of integration observed in these journals.

"I mean if I decide that what's happened to me can be summed up in a sentence, then I can just write that sentence or if I feel that my experience for that day rquires me to write two pages, then I can write two pages. I can write freely without limitations or without expectations."   — Bentley College student

Journals as Data Base

Detailed journals can be a good source of information for analysis by students later in their course. An example of an exercise that uses journals as a data source is given on (See Applying Kob's Learning Cycle, Pg.97) When students know their journals will be used as field notes for later papers, it also encourages them to be thorough and thoughtful in their day-to-day written reflection.

Resource Journals

Some classes combine journal keeping with collecting a wide range of information about the service topic. The resource journal is a notebook filled with the student's written reflection, plus notes from research, articles and news clippings, material from agencies and other relevant resources that the student accumulates during service. These collections can also be used in later synthesis assignments.

"*I did that for all my research and everything like that. So anytime anything pops into my head I try to write it down and try to get something out about it so that I can come back later and draw from that.*"   — *University of Washington student*

EXTRA NOTE: DESIGNING JOURNALS FOR FEEDBACK

Journals can offer the opportunity for written dialogue between instructor and student; feedback was consistently mentioned as critical to students' commitment to thoughtful journal writing. One technique to facilitate this process is to ask students to split each page in half from top to bottom and then to write their own reflections on the left, leaving the right hand column for instructor comment.

"*She had us turn in journal work often and she responded to it in writing. Sometimes they were empathetic responses... I was experiencing a lot of frustration in the beginning... when I would talk about attempts I'd made to rectify a situation... she'd mediate some of the difficulty. It was clear that she was really reading what I was writing... she would say, 'Have you tried this approach?' or 'You may want to try this too.' The feedback was constant and it was always encouraging.*"   — *University of San Diego student*

SOURCE
Students from all schools.

Assembling a Portfolio

What is a service-learning portfolio?

A portfolio is a collection of documents and other forms of evidence of student competencies and achievements, specifically as they relate to learning plan objectives. Portfolios can be used for student and program evaluation and students find them useful when seeking employment. This example is designed as sample instructions for students assembling a portfolio.

What can be included in a portfolio?

♦ Documents you drafted, wrote, or significantly contributed to during preparation.

♦ Written analyses of problems, issues, options or other assessments demonstrating judgment/reasoning.

♦ Finished projects (i.e., videotapes, graphics, charts, spreadsheets, training programs, photos, marketing plans, research results, executive summaries of project reports).

♦ Written evaluations of your work (i.e., performance appraisals, project assessments, critical reviews, letters of commendation or recommendation).

♦ Lists of projects completed, presentations made, training completed, all supported by date, location and organization.

♦ Skill or competency checklists evaluated and completed by a supervisor.

♦ Annotated bibliography of readings related to specific knowledge objectives.

♦ Your resume noting specific professional achievements.

PURPOSE:

Personal Development
♦
Understanding
♦
Application

" *It was basically a really large journal and we would go and research newspaper articles — so we had newspaper articles, the journal, things from the text — different books that we would check into from the library — and things about the topic, different agencies that are service-learning agencies we dealth with... We would write about each article that we read or each book that we read...* "

— University of Washington student

Process

Instructions for Service Internship Portfolio

STEP 1:

Develop a learning plan. Throughout the semester, you should revise your learning plan. As you achieve specific objectives, you should collect evidence of that achievement.

STEP 2:

Organize your portfolio according to knowledge, skill, and professional objectives. In the past, students have used a notebook or an accordion file to hold and organize portfolio items. You may use the portfolio summary form included in your class pak or create your own method of presenting specific objectives and corresponding evidence. In many cases you will need to provide a narrative which explains the level of autonomy you had in completing the final product and the standard to which you achieved a particular objective. Include a copy of your revised learning plan with your portfolio.

STEP 3:

Submit portfolio to your instructor for evaluation.

STEP 4:

Continue to add evidence of your achievements to your portfolio throughout your service career. Your portfolio will prove to be a valuable tool during the job search process. In addition, many organizations are moving toward performance-based assessment for retention, promotion, and development purposes. Concrete evidence of your accomplishments is particularly important in an uncertain and unstable work environment.

How will the portfolio be evaluated?

THE PORTFOLIO WILL BE EVALUATED USING THE FOLLOWING CRITERIA:

◆ To what extent does the learning plan represent an appropriate and sophisticated level of learning? (i.e. learning how to perform a community needs assessment versus learning to file documents at the agency)

◆ To what extent does the learning plan represent a broad range of learning objectives?

◆ Is there evidence for each learning objective?

◆ Does the evidence demonstrate a specified standard of achievement? If not, is there an explanation of why the original standard was not achieved?

◆ Are portfolio items clear evidence that learning has occurred (i.e., an annotated bibliography of readings vs. a list of articles)?

◆ Is the portfolio clearly organized and professionally presented?

A final note...

Although students will submit their final portfolios at the end of the semester, they should be encouraged to begin documenting learning experiences and collecting portfolio items at the beginning of the service-learning experience. Keep in mind that the learning plan and portfolio are integrally linked and will need to be revised as the objectives and activities change.

SOURCE
Woody Caine & Angela
Schmiede, Vanderbilt
University

Reflection Through Letters and Memos

PROCESS

STEP 1

Identify if letters or memos are to be used for reflection or for action.

STEP 2

Identify audience/recipient (self, lobbyists, congressional representatives, community members, agency directors)

STEP 3

After participants have completed the letter of memo, schedule time for reflection afterwards. If letter is written to self, review at a specified time in the future. If letter is sent elsewhere, have participants follow up for a response and reflect on the effectiveness of their message.

VARIATIONS

Problem Analysis Memos

The following is an assignment given to service interns. They must identify a problem and propose a solution to their supervisors.

MEMORANDUM

TO: H & OD Interns

FROM: Dwight Giles, Angela Schmiede, Vera Chatman and Kimberly Bess

DATE: October 25, 1996

RE: Project Proposal Memo / Audience Analysis

It is important to select a topic for your project analysis paper and senior project early in the semester. We would like for each of you to conduct an audience analysis and prepare a one-page memo addressed to your site supervisor which outlines your proposal for a project analysis/senior project topic. The proposal will enable your supervisor to determine if your project is manageable and appropriate to the goals of the organization.

PURPOSE:

Citizenship Development

◆

Understanding

◆

Application

Your memo will serve as an outline for your project analysis paper which is due later in the semester. The first paragraph should begin with your recommended action statement (your proposed solution or senior project), and include a definition of the problem, and a few statements which discuss the history and extent of the problem as well as the current and driving forces. Remember that you want to provide just enough information so that the reader understands your argument and is convinced that this topic should be addressed.

Your second paragraph will include the major objectives and criteria for solving the problem or completing the project you will undertake. The criteria will be used as a checklist for selecting the best solution to this problem or opportunity. You will need to complete and attach an audience analysis matrix to your memo. When formulating a potential solution, it will be important to consider the objectives, values, and limitations associated with the key players and decision makers who are affected by this issue.

The third paragraph will outline how you plan to address this issue. Describe your proposed solution and the methods you will use. Include a statement of the resources you will need as well as any limitations you foresee in addressing the issue. If your proposed senior project does not fit within the project analysis framework, outline your proposed project analysis topic and provide a description of your proposed senior project.

Generally, short memos like yours will not need a summary; however, your project analysis paper should summarize and reinforce your major points. Usually short memos have action-oriented endings (i.e., "I will call you next Monday to discuss the details of my proposal" or "Please review this proposal and provide some feedback by next Friday"). Initial your name at the top of the memo, and when possible, print the memo on letterhead. If you have any questions regarding this assignment, please contact your internship course instructor.

"Ideal Letter of Recommendation"

This assignment is helps students identify goals they might have for their internships before they begin in the field.

STEP 1

Have students visualize for ten minutes the goals they have achieved at the end of the semester.

STEP 2

Give students 20 minutes to write a letter of recommendation for themselves from their supervisors perspective. Make sure that they address knowledge that they have gained, skills they have developed, products they have created or delivered, and issues regarding professionalism.

STEP 3

Have students circle key words in the letter which relate to specific goals they might set.

STEP 4

At the end of the term, have students compare these letters with actual letters of recommendation and their portfolios. Ask them to reflect on how close their accomplishments were to their expectations. Have them identify factors which assisted or prohibited them from achieving goals.

Letter to Self

The following is given to service internship students on the last day of an internship seminar.

STEP 1

Have students reflect on the following for five minutes:

WHAT?
What is the most important thing I have learned during my internship this semester?

SO WHAT?
Why is it important that I learned it?

NOW WHAT?
Given my experience, what are my immediate and long term goals (personal, professional, educational)? Specifically, what are one-year and five-year goals?

STEP 2

Use this format to have students write a letter to themselves. Have students seal the letter in a self-addressed envelope.

STEP 3

At a designated future time (3 months - one year), send students their letters.

STEP 4

If possible, gather students together in a forum (perhaps a second semester course) to reflect on goal progress.

NOTE: This exercise is also effective to use in workshops. Have participants focus on learning gained from the workshop and outline an action plan for putting this learning to use in their own settings.

> SOURCE
> Angela Schmiede, Vanderbilt University.

Integrative Papers

Many students found that writing was the most useful way to integrate their service and learning.

"I think definitely the writing aspect is important. Because I find in my own life that when I write about something, I'm forced to really consider it and analyze it more so than if I'm just talking to a friend about it or something like that. And so I would emphasize that the most — that the learning part of the service-learning is really important and it can only enhance the service portion of it." — University of San Diego student

PURPOSE:

Understanding

◆

Application

◆

Reframing

PROCESS

Most courses used papers as a summative activity for the course; many had students develop a series of products which culminate in a final paper; others had students use their journals as field notes for their final paper.

Because students who are not doing service can do other types of papers, this assignment is easy to use in classes where service is an option rather than a requirement. Students found writing useful, but were critical of courses where a final paper was the only way their service was integrated into the class. The final paper should be the culmination of a series of reflective discussions or assignments, not a substitute for regular integration of the service and the subject matter.

"When you put something down on paper, it helps you straighten out your thoughts. Or helps me anyway. If I am confused about something or bungled up in my mind, if I can get it written down on paper and see exactly what experience I have had... it straightens out my thinking." — East Tennessee State University student

CATEGORIES OF FINAL PAPER ASSIGNMENTS

Problem Solving Papers

Students investigate a social problem related to their community service assignment by defining the problem; analyzing root causes; identifying the stakeholders; identifying alternative policy solutions and recommending a policy to be pursued. This paper is often done in stages with feedback from faculty or other students and students are encouraged to talk to community members and service providers as well as representatives of groups involved in policy making as they plan their recommendation. "Research" is not confined to the library, but includes interviewing experts struggling to deal with the issue in the field.

Theory Application Papers

Students identify a particular theoretical perspective or concept e.g. social penetration theory, and then use the experiences with community service to "test" the theory. Students illustrate key point of the theory with examples — in support or opposition — from their experience. This allows them to anchor their theoretical understanding in experience.

"The two theories that we chose were reasons communication doesn't work. And it sounds so hokie, like I'm just doing it for this interview, but really it was kind of enlightening. We didn't know why communication didn't occur between the two of us and why we weren't able to meet with [anyone at the residence for people living with AIDS] . These were just theories, but it was so neat to say — it could have been this — and who knows what actually happened, but it was so neat to say well, this is the reason why — and it all made sense. And it was, wow this is perfect. Both of them were just these really applicable theories to reasons why communication doesn't work. With the other students in our class they used communication theories why it does work — and it was obvious by their oral presentations that they put a lot of thought into it. The theories they came up with really came close to hitting exactly what was going on with them. . . .It was so neat . . . just to sit there and reading these and say — my God, this might really be what happened. This is so neat to have a real understanding for once instead of saying, 'Oh, he was a flake'. This was reasons why this would happen ."

— University of San Diego student

Case Studies

Case studies can focus on individuals, on the service project itself, or on the agency's role in meeting the needs of community members. In some classes, students read case studies as a model and then created their own.

Service-Learning Self Assessment

Some classes made the final paper an explicit evaluation of the students' service-learning experience using criteria that have been identified for effective experiential learning such as those mentioned in Chapter 1 of this guide. Students discuss their personal growth and critique the program and placement.

Agency Analysis

Students analyze the agency they worked with using appropriate organizational frameworks and evaluation tools. They combine their observations with information about who is served, how policies are made, where funding is obtained and future plans for the organization. The need to create the organizational analysis gives students legitimacy as they seek to meet with key volunteers, board members and staff of the organization. See Organizational Analysis activity on Page 91 for more detail.

"It's just to write a comprehensive paper about the whole experience — like this study and you have to come with a topic — and the topic is just how programs manage inner city youth. And there's different categories to it. Basically it's some of the experiences and the program at different places and how I think, 'This is a great program' — but why? And not just, 'Oh, it's a great program,' but what does this program do for the students who are there?"

— Bentley College student

Book Review

Students read and critique a book related to their community service assignments using the insights garnered during the course of their service. The author's observations and opinions are tested by the student's experience.

SOURCE
Students from all schools.

Organizational Analysis

OVERVIEW

Part of understanding community issues is understanding the nature of the service organizations. Understanding the organization is particularly important if it is connected to a social science course such as an organizational behavior or theory. This can also be a tool to help students understand what is happening in their setting and how to intervene in problem situations in the service placement:

"There were a lot of politics. There was a power play going on within that organization and people trying to subtly assert themselves over others. And discussing different theories of who has power in an organization and studying those in small group behavior class and the organizational behavior class... Well we had to discuss political aspect of organizations and in the seminar, I was able to tie in the concepts that I had learned in the classes that I had taken before through what I was experiencing first hand."

— Vanderbilt University student

Both of the assignments described below will lead up to an organizational analysis paper. The students use either Bolman and Deal's Four Frames (1991) or a focus on the organization's relationship to its external environment as diagnostic tools to help others understand each organization in depth.

PURPOSE:

◆

Understanding

◆

Application

◆

Reframing

ASSIGNMENT PROCESS # 1:
Four Frames Assignment

INSTRUCTIONS

From the following outline of the Bolman and Deal's (1991) *Four Frames* submit answers to at least three (3) questions from each Frame. Try to gather as much information as possible from existing data in the organization. Interview members of the organization for additional information. Answers must be thorough and supported with specific examples. Because not all questions will apply, you will choose which questions are most relevant to that placement site. Be prepared to discuss your organization from each frame perspective.

THE FOUR FRAMES

STRUCTURAL FRAME

The structural frame focuses on who does the work and how the work gets done. When analyzing an organization from the structural perspective, it is useful to ask some of the following questions:

◆ What are the stated goals of the organization? of the department? How much agreement is there on which goals are most important?

◆ How are decisions made? How many people are involved in decision making?

◆ Are explicit policies and rules established for employees? Are roles well-defined or ambiguous? What does the hierarchy of authority look like? What does the organizational chart look like?

◆ How are activities coordinated? Are there many meetings? Are there committees, task forces, etc.?

HUMAN RESOURCE FRAME

The human resource perspective is based on the assumption that organizations exist to meet the needs of people. The following are some useful questions to think about in this frame:

◆ How diverse are the social and educational backgrounds of employees?

◆ How do people feel about their work? Do they feel like they are an essential part of the organization?

◆ What seems to motivate employees? Do they seem happy? What are the existing levels of turnover, grievances, absenteeism? Is the organization unionized?

◆ Do people socialize outside of the workplace?

◆ How well are employees' needs met? (financial, motivational, education & training, day care, opportunities for advancement, responsibility, etc.)

SYMBOLIC FRAME

The symbolic frame looks at the symbolism and culture in an organization. The following questions are useful in viewing the organization from the symbolic perspective:

◆ What do symbols in the organization say about the culture? How is office space arranged? What kind of cars do employees drive?

◆ What visible symbols portray the organization's values? (plaques, pictures, awards, letters, etc.)

◆ What is the history of the organization? Is there a hero or heroine? (founder, president, long-time employee, etc.) Are stories or legends told about the company?

◆ What are the core values of the organization? How well do employees adhere to the core values?

◆ What types of rituals or ceremonies take place? (promotions, holiday parties, organization picnics/outings) How are new employees initiated into the organization?

◆ What type of culture exists? (work hard/play hard, formal/rigid, laid back, etc.)

POLITICAL FRAME

The political frame takes a look at the sources and types of power and authority in organizations and how it affects the organization. Questions to keep in mind are:

◆ Who are the recognized people of power? Is power centralized to one or two people, or is power decentralized throughout the organization?

◆ What is the primary basis of power? (expertise, seniority, charisma, access to resources, fear, authority, etc.) How do people exercise their power?

◆ What issues produce conflict? How is conflict resolved? Are there obvious coalitions within the organization?

◆ How are resources allocated? (money, supplies, employees, office space, etc.) Who controls the allocation of resources?

PROCESSING

Once during the semester, each student is assigned to facilitate class discussion. These discussions will be based on cooperative learning models in which you will be helping one another to learn about and apply organizational theories. Use of creativity is strongly encouraged.

ASSIGNMENT PROCESS #2
The Organization and its External Environment

INSTRUCTIONS

This report should be analytic, integrated and concise. In addition to analyzing how the organization operates internally, it will focus on how your organization responds to factors external to the organization. Your analysis will be a summary of the state of your organization. It should provide a concise overview, from an internal and external perspective, of the challenges the organization currently faces as well as its strengths.

PART 1: THE EXTERNAL ENVIRONMENT

Each student selects an event or a series of events that illustrate how the external environment affects the organization. Examples could include the following:

◆   How political issues surrounding the arena affect the goals of the local union of construction workers.

◆   How legislation regarding immigrants affects the practices of a community center in a Latino community.

◆   How perceptions about scandals related to a national funding source affects donation goal achievement.

Students gather information about these issues and events from local and national news programs and newspapers, trade magazines, competitors' advertisements, etc. Students provide a clear description of the facts related to these issues and events and how they relate to the organization. They should analyze the situation by answering the following questions:

◆   How do key stakeholders perceive these events? How do you think these events will affect you, your co-workers and/or the larger community?

◆   Read the chapter on external environments by Daft and Steers (1986) (*Organization Theory and Design*). — What concepts in these readings help you to understand these events? How would you define your organization in terms of environmental stability and certainty?

◆   Based on the above, if you were a key decision maker in your organization, what would you do to address and control environmental change in this situation?

PART 2: THE ORGANIZATION

Students identify two important consistencies or inconsistencies which exist in the organization. In other words, they describe the most critical strengths or weaknesses identified from the perspective of either Daft and Steers (1986) or Bolman and Deal (1991). They should identify possible causes and effects of the issue cited and discuss how the organization should address these issues.

PART 3: SUMMARY

Summarize the current state of the organization:

◆   Does it exist in a certain or uncertain environment? A stable or unstable environment?

◆   How stable is the internal environment?

SOURCE
Vanderbilt University,
    University of Tennessee
    & University of Colorado

Critical Questions

One of the most important of the 4 C's of effective reflection is Challenge — reflection must push students to think on a more complex level, to evaluate assumptions and stereotypes, and to consider opposing viewpoints. Any reflection activity — regardless of the methods involved — needs to challenge service-learners; and posing critical questions is a powerful way to add this challenging element to written assignments as well as discussion and other exercises.

"For the first couple of weeks she gave us little prompts like... 'What is your first impression?' 'What was different than you first expected?' 'How did you feel about the people?' ...We had to analyze a few of the situations according to sociological perspectives that we learned like conflict theory ...and we had to define our problem as a social problem."

— University of Washington student

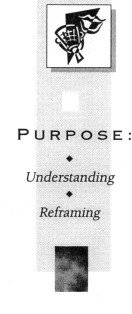

PURPOSE:

◆

Understanding

◆

Reframing

PROCESS

Here the teacher or group leader poses critical questions about the student's writing or oral presentations. Often these are the standard critical questions that teachers write on the margins of essays and papers, frequently in red. These questions are designed to urge the student to think twice about assumptions and generalizations, deepen the reflective thinking process, and consider other points of view — particularly those that are radically different from their own.

"I thought my program made sense. And then the acting director comes along and he asked me some questions about — what's this and what's this and what's that — and I just had to stop and actually think and redesign the program so that the goals and the objectives and the strategies and the outcomes — they're all linked — there's no loopholes. And with all this - it wasn't really there on paper per se. It was there in my head. And so I had to stop and think and rework the entire program itself."

— Bentley College student

In general, critical questions will focus on a few key categories. Several of these categories and questions to address them are included on the next page.

DEEPENING PERSONAL EXPLORATION

◆   Did you have an emotional reaction to that comment/event? What was the first thing that came to your mind?

◆   Did this experience remind you of any similar experiences in the past?

◆   Were you proud of or disappointed in your reaction/the way you handled the situation?

◆   What surprises you about what you have written here?

SEEKING EVIDENCE TO DEFEND CLAIMS

◆   How do you know that? What background reading or research leads you to that opinion?

◆   How **sure** are you about this?

◆   How could we have obtained more data on the subject?

DEALING WITH DIFFERING VIEWPOINTS

◆   What life experience of your own has led to you hold that point of view? How do you think individuals with a different life experience would feel? Have you spoken about this with anyone?

◆   What is the opposing viewpoint to your opinion? Why do you think other people believe that?

◆   How do we decide which position is correct?

EVALUATING EFFECT ON THE COMMUNITY

◆   Who benefited from this effort?

◆   Who might oppose such a project? Could the community suffer any negative consequences as a result of this project?

◆   What will the long-term impact of your efforts be? In 5 years, will your accomplishments remain intact?

"We had about six headings you had to talk about like the history of our program and what theory it fell under, how it was a social problem. We were supposed to do it throughout the entire thing. Things like if you had a discussion with someone while at the shelter and decided to write about it in your journal, then you might talk about how this person had run away because of a breakdown in family, like drug abuse or something like that. And talk about it in that perspective." — University of San Diego student

SOURCE
Students from all schools

Applying Kolb's Learning Cycle

USING REFLECTION PAPERS TO INCREASE THE LEARNING POTENTIAL IN SERVICE-LEARNING

Students are often asked to keep journals or to prepare papers dealing with their experience in service-learning as a way to reflect on that experience and as a way for supervisors to monitor and assess their learning. Students sometimes have difficulty making these assignments really useful in the learning process and often don't see the connections between their experience and the formal theory and concepts presented in their more didactic course work.

David Kolb's (1984) learning cycle (See Chapter 3 for related information) provides a model which has proven useful as a way to structure the writing process so students are led to seek more specific and informed explanations of the organizational dynamics they see in their sites (which can be found in the theory provided by instructors and text material).

A coherent Reflection Paper format can be based on Kolb's four basic phases of the learning process:

1. *A concrete experience.*

2. *A time to reflect on the experience.*

3. *An opportunity to apply concepts, models and theories to explain the experience.*

4. *An opportunity to test, evaluate, and reconceptualize one's understanding of the experience.*

PURPOSE:

Understanding

◆

Application

The Reflection Paper is a strong method to encourage students to apply the concepts in the text and lecture material to their own experience. It has worked well, for example, as a way to help more students make the leap from more superficial and idiosyncratic explanations of group dynamics to more educated and insightful understanding of the processes at work in group situations.

Advantages:

• Provides more structure so students are led through a more complete learning cycle.

• Provides *'prompts'* (questions) to stimulate thinking and help make connections from theory to practice.

• Provides more structure for the instructors to evaluate students' written products connected with the service-learning course.

• Provides a vehicle for an instructor to assess what concepts need to be reinforced and taught.

• Form can be modified for use in several ways (different written assignments with slightly different objectives) during the service-learning experience and can provide an integrating element in the academic part of a service-learning experience.

Disadvantages:

• Can require considerable instructor time to evaluate and give written feedback.

• Can inhibit some students from expressing what they view as their important learning.

PROCESS

The generic structure for this paper is provided in Sidebar Format on this and the next page. Students are encouraged to use their journal entries to begin the reflection process in Phase 1, Concrete Experience. Conceptual elements in Abstract Conceptualization can be furnished from readings, group discussion, or previous reflection papers.

Reflection Papers are usually five typed pages in length. Students are taught the generic model in class by focusing on and writing about a critical event early in their field work. They then complete four Reflection Assignments which use the format over the course of the class or service-learning experience. Each assignment has a slightly different emphasis and poses different questions to help students develop each of the four phases of the paper. Among the topics are stages of service, organizations external environments, goal setting and accomplishment and social issues. Each instructor chooses the topics and assigns the appropriate readings.

SAMPLE CONTENT

The Kolb cycle can be used to structure papers on almost any topic of relevance to the service-learning experience. The following shows the flow of a paper assignment focusing on Community Partnerships.

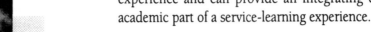

Reflection Paper Format...
...and Criteria for Evaluation

PHASE 1.
Concrete Experience

Description of specific behaviors which occurred during the incident or facts related to a particular situation. Use names, dates, places and be objective.

◆ Level of detail and specificity.
◆ Include descriptions of your behaviors and the behaviors of others (verbal and nonverbal behavior).

PHASE 2.
Reflective Observation

Personal reflection about the event(s).

◆ Your thoughts and feelings about the incident(s)/situation.
◆ Your perceptions of others' thoughts and feelings about the events.
◆ Your perceptions of how this event has affected individuals in your service setting and why.

Reflecting on Community Partnerships

This framework can be used for written or oral discussion reflection with partners in the community. It is designed to help individuals "reframe" the way in which they view community partnerships.

CONCRETE EXPERIENCE

Community Partnerships in service-learning can generally be defined as relationships among the following parties:

- Educational institutions
- Citizens
- Agencies/Organizations
- Students/Volunteers

Describe a situation in your service experience where you have been in a community partnership. Describe the interaction you had with the other party. Include descriptions of verbal and nonverbal behaviors. Be objective in your descriptions.

REFLECTIVE OBSERVATION

- What was your reaction to this event?
- What were you seeking in this relationship?
- What do you think the other party was seeking in this relationship?
- What assumptions did you make about the other individual(s)?
- How do you think the other party felt about the interaction? What assumptions do you think the other party made about you?

ABSTRACT CONCEPTUALIZATION

Given your experience and observations, how would you explain the nature of this partnership? In particular, what models or concepts might help explain the dynamics and outcomes of this relationship? For example:

- What influence does **culture** have on the nature of this relationship?

PHASE 3.
Abstract conceptualization

Relationship between the event(s) observed and experienced, and the theories and concepts studied in class.

- What theories in the reading and material presented in class help you to explain and understand the situation itself and/or the dynamics you saw and experienced?

- Where might your assumptions at the time or afterward have been shortsighted or faulty?

- Given the situation as you understand it, do you have any critiques of the applied theories or conceptual models?

PHASE 4.
Active Experimentation

How does this learning relate to other situations you might encounter in the future?

- How can you test your new assumptions about yourself, others or the organization?

- This learning might apply to what kinds of situations in the future?

- Next time, what would you try in a similar situation?

- What influence does **power** have on the nature of this relationship?

- How might **assumptions** you made be faulty, or **stereotypes** you had be shortsighted?

- How does your definition of "service" impact your behavior and goals in this relationship? How does society define "service" and how does it compare to your definition? How do you think the other party defines "service"?

ACTIVE EXPERIMENTATION

- How might this learning impact the way in which you relate with community partners in the future?

- How has it impacted your definition of "service"?

- What can you do to become more aware of cultural differences and how factors in the external environment impact service experiences?

- Next time, what would you try in a similar situation? What opportunities exist in this relationship?

USE IN A SERVICE INTERNSHIP PROGRAM

This format is very effective in a semester's internship course. Students are required to keep a more traditional daily journal in which they record the events which serve as the background for the Reflection Papers.

SERVICE-LEARNING APPLICATIONS

Such structured reflective journaling can be used in service-learning in several ways. It can be used to reflect on small group dynamics, organizational structure or the dynamics of a community service project. It can also be used to enhance the learning about a community problem (e.g. homelessness), the nature of service, and accompanying policy issues. Reflection Papers provide a means to integrate readings, concepts and students' personal experiences. We have found that they eliminate student complaints about the drudgery of daily journaling, especially over long periods of time.

SOURCE
Pat Arnold, Vanderbilt University

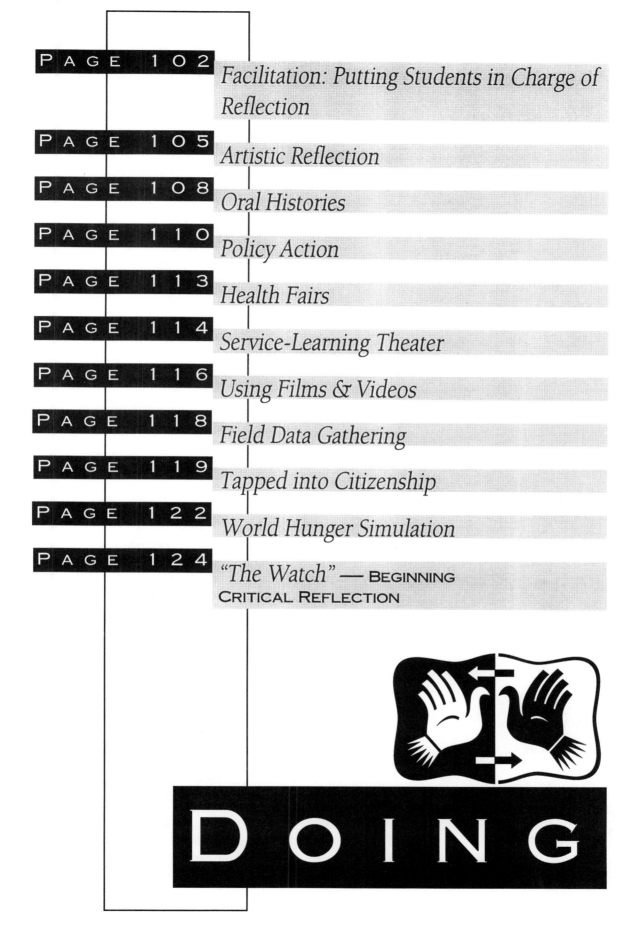

DOING

Facilitation: Putting Students in Charge of Reflection

Giving students responsibility for conducting reflection sessions is a powerful way to encourage analysis and synthesis of their experience. It is also a great chance for students to practice facilitation as a part of their broader leadership development.

"The facilitations have been really helpful. Because they are so hard to do and you want to do a really good job, so you kind of think more about creative ways that you can bring your service organization to the group and make it interesting and lively and refreshing."

— University of Colorado student

PROCESS

Students identified a number of approaches to student-led reflection. On the facing page you will find several exercises that students mentioned in conjunction with student-facilitated reflection. However, any of the activities outlined in Chapter 4 can be organized as student-led reflection.

BASIC TRAINING

There are several risks in putting students in charge of facilitation. The service-learning practitioner must give up the conflict-management role to the student in charge. And students who are not experienced facilitators may feel overwhelmed by the task. These risks can easily be minimized by providing students with some basic training in facilitation skills. Some of the most important elements to consider are these:

♦ Watch the time.

Plan time limits for each segment of the agenda, and inform the group of these time limits. Appoint a time keeper to remind the group of progress.

♦ Establish "Group Norms"

PURPOSE:

♦

*Connecting
with Others*

♦

Understanding

♦

Application

...at the beginning of any session — these are "Ground Rules" that the group brainstorms, evaluates and agrees to abide by during discussion (i.e. "Don't interrupt." "Use gender inclusive language." "Avoid side conversations."). The group agrees by consensus to the Group Norms, and everyone is responsible for holding each other accountable. In a classroom setting, or in a group with regular meetings, these can be established at the beginning of the semester and reviewed (and revised if necessary) at the beginning of each individual session.

♦ Validate everyone's opinions and contributions.

For shared group experiences to be meaningful, each individual must feel that there is a "Safe Space" within that group — that he or she can be honest about feelings and thoughts without the risk of being attacked, treated disrespectfully or alienated as a result. If someone says something that obviously angers or offends other people in the group, the facilitator can ask follow up questions to clarify the intended meaning and to find out what life experiences have led that individual to the conclusion voiced. Be sure to affirm that individual's right to the opinion, based on his or her life experience.

♦ Be Challenging.

Protecting the "Safe Space" within a group does not mean that a facilitator can abandon this critical part of the 4 C's. While affirming someone's right to an opinion and listening carefully to his or her story, the facilitator can also challenge any assumptions or generalizations that may have led to a weak link between some life experience and a certain view of the world. See Critical Questions (Page 95) for specific questions that may be of use.

♦ Be Neutral.

The facilitator's role is to ensure that everyone has a chance to contribute — not to gain access to your own personal soap box. If your views on a certain subject are so strong that you are unable to remain objective and quiet during that discussion, you need to trade roles with someone who can be neutral.

PREPARATION

Once students have received some training and tips on facilitation technique, they should be given their assignments with extra time to spare to allow for adequate preparation. Students may benefit from some one-on-one time with the professor or trainer during which they can "walk through" the session they are planning and receive feedback and specific pointers. Requiring students to submit a written agenda (including time allocation for each section of the session) will also help to ensure that the planning process is a manageable learning process.

SAMPLE WAYS TO STRUCTURE A SESSION

Some examples were specifically mentioned by student interviewees:

Free Form Reflection

Students are assigned times where they are responsible for facilitating reflection, but the focus and method are left entirely to them. Students mentioned organizing panels of speakers, creating simulations, doing skits or role plays and facilitating discussions.

"*Every day a different student would be the leader — we were doing power issues and the person brought in all the ingredients to make chocolate chip cookies and just said, "Go." And watched the group make chocolate chip cookie dough and then we discussed the symbolism and who did what role, who sat back and who took charge and that was never assigned. That was what a student thought of... those were the most effective things."*

— University of Colorado student

Theory into Practice

Students are assigned theories from the course and asked to lead a session where they help the group apply the theory to their diverse experiences in the field.

Jig Saw

Students are assigned different reading related to the service experience and facilitate discussions where they share the perspective they have explored.

"But I really liked anything like that. I was required to do that as a student leader. I facilitated for my class. I did it for the student leaders this semester. And it's good. I usually like doing reflections with myself. I think I do a good job at it, but this was a different way of looking at it. It posed a challenge for myself and I know a lot of other people. So, it was a great reflection." — University of San Diego student

FACILITATING AS SERVICE

Advanced students can also facilitate community workshops or sessions on campus designed to recruit new participants.

"This weekend I'm helping to facilitate a workshop on labeling — part of our new connections program — I'll be facilitating the workshop with 7 other people — our topic is labeling, so we'll be there presenting and it should be really exciting and fun and very informative." — University of San Diego Student

EVALUATION

Facilitation is a skill developed through a great deal of practice — and with a great deal of training and feedback necessary for improvement. Students should have the opportunity to receive written feedback (from the professor or trainer and from fellow students) as well as oral evaluation, perhaps in the form of a "debriefing" with the trainer immediately following the session that he or she facilitates.

SOURCE
Students at Bentley College, University of Colorado, University of Washington and Vanderbilt University.

Artistic Reflection

Expressing feelings is often the first step in the process of reflecting on service. For many students artistic expression is a powerful method for communicating feelings and synthesizing the meaning of their experience.

PURPOSE:

Self-Development
◆
Connecting With Others
◆
Citizenship Commitment

"*I think some people see me coming in for a critique in art and they think, 'Oh no, here she is again with another social problem'... but pretty much everything I've done has got something to do with something that I've experienced. On the reservation things that have come up about class and race and all that... And photography, when I first got back from the reservation I was doing things on conditions there... I've done a lot of things on how maybe we've treated a lot of things on the reservation and just a lot of things with connections to others — like I've used quotes from Chief Seattle in the print or something that I've done. . . I don't think it's something that I'm seeking out so much but it's something that had become such a big aspect of my life that I just can't help but do it.*"

— University of Colorado student

PROCESS

A variety of projects combine service experience and artistic expression. For students who are confident of some sort of artistic talent, the process will be natural. Most individuals, however, have developed a negative feeling towards their own creations over the years. It is important to affirm the value of individuality and creativity and to ease students into the artistic process. Following are several ideas of artistic projects that translate into effective reflection.

Community of Ideas Mural

At one of the regional Learn and Serve America conferences a visual artist worked as discussions took place, capturing in drawings the ideas of participants on a mural to convey a community of service. A similar mural could be created with each student or student team contributing images. The mural could grow chronologically throughout the service or could be used to synthesize what students feel they have learned about community or service. It can also be used before service as a form of '*visualization*'. The mural could be a collage, a finger painting, or any type of more traditional art.

Artistic Journal

Artistic expression can be included in journals or a specific art journal can be created in which students express feelings and ideas about their service. Students are asked to choose a creative medium such as drawing, poetry or music and develop 'creative' entries to their artistic journal from time to time during their service. A group can also create an artistic portfolio.

Song Lyrics

Creating a song can be a fun and powerful way to conclude a semester of service. A common refrain can be used and each student or team of students can write a verse capturing something important about their service. One group did this with the tune from Yankee Doodle.

"I know there was one group that made us all cry the most was the group that studied youth in crisis and they had spent some time at a runaway shelter and a home for teenagers and young children and crisis hotlines and all these amazing and powerful things that they had been through. They wrote a song about it and hearing that song and singing along with it and learning the words, it became our song, and it became a symbol of all that we wanted to do and all that we had learned."

— Vanderbilt University student

Poetry Round Robin

Here is one way to use poetry with a group of service-learning participants. After a project, one person writes one to two lines of reflection on the experience. The next person continues the poem with one or two lines and then folds over the paper so that only his or her written reflection is showing. The poem is passed to each participant who can only see the work of the person immediately preceding him or her. The poem is then read to the group.

Photography and Video Taping

Photo journals and video tapes about the service experience are useful for helping students plan and think about the meaning of their experience. And they can also be useful to help students present information about their service to others.

"I know one of the groups in our change project put together this slide show and they've gone around and they've been trying to talk about what [we've] been doing. And I think

that's probably a really good way to have further reflection. Because what you're doing as far as action is great, but for further consciousness raising and also understanding what it means to you to work together in groups and put together things for either your class or other classes on campus or just a whole thing on service-learning at the campus — I think would be a really good source of reflection, and I think it would be really community building too. " — University of Colorado student

S O U R C E :
Students at the University of Colorado and the University of San Diego

Oral Histories

In some service settings, students may have the opportunity to record oral histories of community members; in most settings, there is at least the chance to interview service providers. These oral histories can provide helpful background information about communities and organizations, new insights into service-learning related issues, and a chance to forge a closer relationship with a community member. In many situations, the process of recording oral histories can in itself become a community-service project: recorded oral histories become part of the written record of a community, an organization or a region; and they are a useful contribution to make to a museum, a library or a community center.

PROCESS

STEP 1

Based upon class content, each student develops objectives for the oral history session with a community member:

◆ What would you most like to know about this individual's background?

◆ Who else does this individual know? Are there organizations or people that you would like to learn more about?

◆ What might this person be most interested in sharing?

◆ What information would be of most service to local community agencies and organizations?

◆ What information would be of most historical value? Are there stories that only this individual can tell? Which of these should be recorded for future generations?

Based on these objectives, the student will develop a set of interview questions for the community member to answer.

PURPOSE:

◆

*Connecting
with Others*

◆

Understanding

STEP 2

Each student interviews a community member — in person — recording the individual's life story and commentary on cassette or paper.

STEP 3

Students compile or transcribe the community member's words and stories, adding pictures, newspaper articles and other memorabilia that the community member might be willing to donate to the project. Involving the interviewee in this process can be an additional opportunity for reflection and relationship building.

STEP 4

Students prepare the oral history for donation to whatever agencies and individuals the interviewee chooses. Local museums, archives and libraries as well as historians, professors and community agencies may be able to use the oral histories for research or maintain them as historical documents. Other students will certainly benefit from a presentation of the oral histories, and family members of the interviewee may enjoy attending and participating in a session with the students following the presentation. The interviewee and family may also like to keep a copy of the oral history as a keepsake.

"I get to know them and talk to them, incredible. You see what they've been through, and you say, 'Wow.' It's very helpful cause they give you the stories they have, it's incredible. They're so strong, mentally. After what they have been through, you know. So, you just say, 'Wow.' Even if you go down whatever, there's a way out."

— Bentley College student

S O U R C E :
University of Washington,
  University of San Diego, and
  Bentley College students

Policy Action

Students who participate in service-learning projects and reflective analysis of the social problems they encounter through those projects will begin to develop ideas of how their service to the community can be improved in terms of long-term impact. They develop a motivation to work in conjunction with community agencies to develop projects to bring about change in public policy affecting the community agencies with which they work.

PURPOSE:

◆

Citizenship Development

◆

Understanding

◆

Application

These students are following through with Kolb's cycle, beginning to apply the theories that they have developed out of observation and experience. Application facilitates transfer of learning, and following their involvement in policy action projects, these students may be even more likely to continue to be active participants in their communities.

PROCESS: INVOLVING STUDENTS FOR THE FIRST TIME

Less experienced students can be involved in a well structured project for a community group. The facilitator should work with community groups to identify policy related tasks such as performing a community needs assessment; assessing available housing options for the homeless; or providing background research for a group working to change laws.

"*One thing that we did one semester that I thought was really interesting was that we did a needs assessment. The one that I worked on was in education. We went around to different school and we had different topics that we wanted to assess... So, we went to schools and we participated in classrooms and we talked to teachers and counselors and principals. We looked at curriculum and we did a whole proposal based on those needs... And then that's where we decided to — we had to come out with a change project and we had to come out with a whole strategy on what were the needs, and what was wrong with the situation and how we could solve that.*"

— University of Colorado student

PROCESS: SUPPORTING EXPERIENCED STUDENTS' INITIATIVES

Experienced student service-learners are often drawn to projects which are designed to create programs or influence policy. Faculty members can facilitate this process by helping them identify issues they want to work on and groups to work with. Students with more experience in policy action may be able to link an Organizational Analysis (see page 91) assignment with a Policy Action project — as a part of the student's assessment of the organization's needs, he or she can look at how policy, laws and other external factors affect the organization's mission. The student can then work with agency representatives to develop strategies to address these external factors.

"*We wrote a proposal... worked with a counselor in Boston. It didn't pass or anything and they keep working on it. But that was — our teacher was really excited about it too. Here we were taking real life stuff and trying to make a law... all of us working on it had worked with homeless people for two years and we were really into it. And we understood that there are people out there that can't make those kinds of decisions. So we had to do research on it and we found out that Chicago and New York had tried it. And New York actually took a person off the street and that person sued them and won. So that's an example of trying to do the right thing, but not getting the results. It's another thing that didn't work out in our favor, but it was something good, because here we are in a law class, but we're making it pertain to stuff that we're really interested in and we had a say and helped out a counselor a lot with our opinions and our experiences. Instead of just doing a basic research project on a topic in law, we were actually trying to make something happen.*"

— Bentley College student

SUGGESTED POLICY ACTION PROJECTS

◆

Research history of policy affecting a grassroots community initiative

◆

Interview local candidates to find allies in the public arena

◆

Launch a letter-writing effort to encourage responsible action on the part of your congressional representatives

◆

Compose letters to the editor of your local paper

"*We are working on increasing the individual donors and fund-raising [for a community service group whose seed grant had run out] I talked to marketing professors here at school and other marketing students; I haven't gotten into marketing classes yet, but that's my major. So I'm getting their opinions on how to help and I'll be talking to other people at other shelters to find out what they do, so I can help my project... when I heard the chance to work at the food project and work with my major and learning more stuff about what I want to do later in life, I jumped at that chance.*"

— University of San Diego student

SOURCE:
Students at Bentley College, University of Colorado, University of Washington and Vanderbilt University

Health Fairs

The Health Fair is one way that students can combine the reflection, education and service components of service-learning in one event. A Health Fair gathers medical professionals and students together, providing valuable medical services and information to community members who ordinarily may not have regular access to quality health care. In addition, the planning process as well as the community interaction allows service-learners the chance to gather information about the community in which they work and to reflect with community members, other students, and professionals about the issues that affect the health care situation in the area.

PURPOSE:

◆

Citizenship Development

◆

Application

PROCESS

THE STUDENT ROLE

Students — as individuals or in small groups — select a health-related topic and develop a research project on the subject. The end result should be an interactive display, perhaps with brochures or hand-outs to distribute to community members. The students then coordinate a health fair at some central location, school or community center, consisting of a series of informational displays and health screening booths.

"We had a health fair. We got a lot of different professionals from all aspects of health care and they set up booths and we were in charge of that and doing the publicity — we learned a lot from that ourselves. More than just somebody who's passing by and seeing it and going through it. Because we knew what we wanted to get out of it and that was really structured. We'd go in and say, 'I want to ask you a question about this, and you'd sit down and talk about it. And disassociate yourself from running the health fair and actually be able to go through and enjoy it, be a participant."

— East Tennessee State University student

CONNECTING WITH HEALTH CARE PROVIDERS

In addition to the informational booths designed and staffed by student service-learners, stations that screen blood pressure, cholesterol levels and other medical factors can be set up by recruiting local health care providers or volunteer doctors and nurses from your college or university.

SOURCE:
East Tennessee State University and Vanderbilt students

Service-Learning Theater

Debriefing large groups can pose problems. Service-learning theater adds variety while engaging students actively in planning, presenting and discussing their 'plays.' If written critical incidents or journals (See Page 78) are used as the basis for the presentations, the exercise also reinforces the previous written reflection.

PURPOSE:

◆

Understanding

◆

Application

"And we actually did a role play and did almost like a performance of the conflict and analyzed it with our [group] and then opened it up for a big discussion. I think taking conflicts like that and letting the students have creative freedom with it were really effective, because we learned... it was very educational, but at the same time we were able to use our analysis from our own experiences in INVST prior to that like an analysis of how they work, was it successful, what could have been done differently in terms of leadership skills and we were able to incorporate that, too."

— University of Colorado student

PROCESS

STEP 1

Students record 'critical incidents' each week during their service. This may be part of a journal or a separate assignment. Use the critical incident form on the facing page to gather consistent information each week.

STEP 2

Collect the critical incident forms and identify several that relate to theories and concepts relevant to the course of study. For example, you might select incidents involving formal and informal power structures, blocked communication, racial or gender conflicts, discretion in providing service to community members, agenda setting, or enforcement of norms, laws or rules.

STEP 3

Select between three and five specific incidents which relate to and illustrate different concepts of interest that are particularly important or timely topics for discussion.

STEP 4

Ask the author of each incident to work with a small group of peers to create a brief role play or skit based on the incident and illustrating the target concepts. Students are seated in a circle and each group presents their skit in the center of the circle. Discussion of the incident proceeds with students asking questions of the players, sharing similar incidents or issues from their own service and explicitly identifying how the events illustrate key concepts under study.

CRITICAL INCIDENT RECORD
(Complete one each week of service-learning placement)

Student Name:_____

Service Site:_____

Choose an event (from your service-learning field work) that took place this week — that you either observed or in which you participated. It should be an event in which a decision was made, a conflict occurred, a change was made, or a problem was resolved (the "problem" might be a difficult decision you had to make on your own or a problem involving many members of the organization). Describe the event and how it was resolved or concluded. Identify those individuals involved in the event. What is their role in the organization? Why was the issue important to them? Who was influential in the outcome and why? Describe the communication process that took place. If the event is a decision you made, why did you decide as you did? Based on this event, what conclusions can you draw about people and organizations?

Week Incident took place:_____

Description: (Use back and/or additional pages as needed)_____

_____

"*...Last semester I worked with somebody and we did this example of how the disunity of groups totally prevents any furthering of the cause and doing it through role playing incorporating the whole class has been sort of the pinnacle. We got to express what we were doing in front of the whole class, which because they've all been there, but they're not doing what I'm doing . . gives me a forum because I know they are interested to talk about it and when they ask questions or they want to know what's going on, then it gets me to clarify what I'm doing.*"

— University of Colorado student

S O U R C E :
University of Colorado students and Janet Eyler, Vanderbilt University

PURPOSE:

♦

Understanding

Using Films, Videos and Documentaries for Reflection

Films, videos and documentaries offer some of the same information that reading materials provide and yet add interest and variety to the service-learning reflection process.

"*Well the format at the Motivation Education seminar, when they first came in they had given us different statistics about inner city children and then they started showing us videos — because they tape everything they do — so, I think actually being able to watch it and see it — that's the format they use. They use a lot of visuals, video tapes and stuff. So, I think that really helped me.*"

— Clark Atlanta University student

PROCESS

STEP 1

Identify objective for using film or documentary. For example, the video can be used to educate participants on issues such as homelessness, drug abuse, or government policy. Use of multiple videos can be used to show different perspectives on a social issue. Videos can also be used as an icebreaker during training sessions.

STEP 2

Determine if you will use the entire film or certain clips. Make sure that copyright is not violated.

STEP 3

After viewing the video, participants should reflect on what they saw either through writing (such as a take-home exam) or discussion.

Sample Questions for Reflection

♦ What is the primary message of the video?

♦ How did the video make you feel? How do you think the participants in the video felt?

♦ What did you learn from the video?

• What concepts/theories discussed in class or readings can be used to explain what happens in the video?

• How well did the actors portray this issue in a realistic way? Why do you think so?

• What are the driving and restraining forces related to this issue?

• What is the government currently doing to address this issue?

• What do you think should be done to address this issue?

"We saw some films and some documentaries on — especially on homelessness, we saw a few about homeless teenagers. That was before I really started getting involved with the shelter. I think that helped. That helped reflect on the problem more." — University of Washington student

SUGGESTED SOURCES:

News segments (current events)

◆

C-Span

◆

Documentaries

◆

TV Series: [*My So Called Life* (adolescent issues), *NYPD Blue* (crime, violence, social issues), *ER* (health/social issues, group dynamics of a team)]

◆

Movies: [*Grand Canyon* (social issues, drug use, crime, violence, effects on families), *Matewan* (labor history — working people's issues)

SOURCE:
Clark Atlanta University,
University of Washington and
Vanderbilt University students

Field Data Gathering

Field Data Gathering is similar to the Oral History (See page 108) activity described earlier in this section and can be adapted to develop portraits of neighborhoods, organizations and communities. Field Data Gathering can also be used as a project similar to Policy Action (See page 110).

"...We're split up into groups analyzing social services and education in (our community) and it's one of the teacher's projects to get us to know our community better. And so we're doing participant observation and we're interviewing people who are involved, getting a picture of those two areas of service in the (local) community. And from there we're writing up the analysis of the information we gathered."

— University of Colorado student

PROCESS

Sometimes community groups or agencies need specific kinds of data that can be gathered from observation or interviewing. In some instances the data gathering is a form of service or can accompany direct service.

In other situations studying the community or community issues can be part of the class work as long as it is done without exploiting community members in the data gathering process. The exercise also helps students to gather contextual information related to the service setting.

"I think if you write right away it's great because you remember everything. You shouldn't take them in with you and be writing stuff down, but right away — and our professor was like, 'I want to know the smell of the place, I want to know what the place looks like. I want to know everything. What someone said to you.' So, it was very easy to take the field notes."

— Bentley College student

PURPOSE:

◆

Understanding

SOURCE:

University of Colorado and Bentley College students (See also Timothy Stanton, "Discovering the Ecology of Human Organizations: Exercises for Field Study Students" in Suelzle and Borzak, 1981.)

Tapped Into Citizenship: A Simulation

The student who shared this experience saw it as a quick way to demonstrate the power of norms and status within society. It was designed to begin a discussion about assumptions about the rules we live by and to make volunteers more sensitive to assumptions they make about the 'right way to do things.'

PROCESS

SETTING THE TONE

It is important that the facilitator adopt a very serious tone during this exercise. If possible, even act a little irritable beforehand. It helps the impact of the exercise if the students feel that they should be careful not to anger the facilitator.

STEP 1

Have the group get into a circle; don't explain the purpose of the exercise; approach it as if it were an energizer or icebreaker.

STEP 2

Demonstrate the position that they will be assuming (crouching down in a deep knee bend, balanced only on the balls of their feet) Stress that during the exercise their eyes must be kept closed, that the exercise must be done in absolute silence, and that no other part of their bodies (hands, etc.) may touch the ground at any time — balls of the feet only! Then instruct them to assume the demonstrated position and close their eyes.

PURPOSE:

◆

Understanding

◆

Reframing

STEP 3

Read the rules clearly and in a deep voice if at all possible. Be serious — do not laugh, even if the students are laughing. If you see someone cheating, walk nearer that person and state the rules loudly in his/her direction; this usually straightens them out. But don't actually *enforce* the rules in any way. The hope is that they will eventually rescue each other, even if this involves "cheating". Anything that happens will make for a good discussion.

THE RULES

"*Rule Number One:*   Don't cheat.

Rule Number Two: If I tap you once, repeat the rules.

Rule Number Three: If I tap you twice, stand up, but keep your eyes closed.

Rule Number Four: If I tap you three times, you can do whatever you want.*"

STEP 4

After you've repeated the rules several times, start tapping one or two people on the head (ONCE) to make them repeat the rules. Keep tapping people once, and continue to repeat the rules yourself so as to keep up a rhythm of repetition and chanting.

STEP 5

Don't tap anyone more than once until you've observed everyone struggling to keep their balance and experiencing some substantial discomfort. Then, slowly, start tapping (one person at a time) a few people twice, and, eventually, three times. Some students, when tapped three times, will begin to torment the remaining crouchers by tapping them once, some will wander off and take some "selfish" time, and some will eventually think to rescue their companions by either ending the exercise or tapping the remaining crouchers three times.

ENDING THE EXERCISE

If you've tapped half of the group three times, and they still haven't started rescuing the others, go ahead and end the exercise yourself and sit down to discuss it. Otherwise, let the participants rescue all of their comrades, thus ending the exercise.

"*What happened is a few people tapped people who were near them 3 times, but never did they go around to tap everybody. And I heard about a workshop once where the people who were tapped 3 times left and went to a bar and some people were left squatting for 3 hours. And then afterwards you talk about it and ask 'does this happen in society?'. And of course, you draw it out and ask questions and challenge... and you ask 'what are you going to do? Are you going to stand around and watch the people suffer or are you going around and tap other people and let them do whatever they want... the real challenge was when you are doing service, are we tapping people once, twice or three times?*"

— Vanderbilt University student

FACILITATOR'S POINTS FOR DISCUSSION

- *How did you feel when you were crouching?* [Draw out discomfort, pain, suffering]

- *Who was tapped once? What was the effect of repeating the rules?* [Hypnotic, like being in a cult, brainwashing, chaotic/confusing]

◆ *Who was tapped twice? How did it feel to stand up? Were you comfortable even though your eyes were closed?*

◆ *Who was tapped three times? What did you do? Why? What could you have done? What kept you from doing it?*

◆ *Who has the power in this exercise? How do you define power?* [Students usually state that the facilitator has power — ask *why? Who gave me that power? Who else has power?*]

REVISIT THE SIGNIFICANCE OF EACH RULE

◆ *What did "Don't Cheat"\" mean in the exercise?* Think about societal rules — Who makes the rules? Encourage them to think about rules not only in terms of laws but also in terms of norms. Who has the power to change the rules in society? Did anyone question the rules of the exercise? Why not? (Point out that tapping others three times once you'd been tapped didn't even require "cheating" — you could rescue people (eventually) even without changing the laws of this oppressive situation.

◆ *What did "Repeat the Rules" mean in the exercise?* Think about socialization into the status quo, blind acceptance.

◆ *What did "Do Whatever You Want" mean in the exercise?* Who in society is usually "tapped three times" and able to do whatever they want. How can we as citizens take advantage of our own personal power to tap other people three times (either within the rules or by changing the rules)?

CONCLUSION

Once the specifics of the simulation are discussed all sorts of symbolic links can be made to service-learning experiences. Explore particularly how our behavior is shaped by rules and norms, why we rarely question those norms, how people come to be in positions of privilege or authority and the different ways people use those advantages. This exercise presents all sorts of discussion possibilities and can be tied into almost any subject. Most important, however, is the moment of truth when it occurs to the participants (either during or after the exercise) that they have the power as citizens to halt oppression in the exercise and in society. Who has the courage to do it?

SOURCE:
Vanderbilt Alternative Spring Break

World Hunger Simulation

This simulation provides a structured experience that demonstrates some of the dynamics of inequity in resource distribution as it tends to function in the global economy.

PROCESS

The simulation takes place in the context of a normal meal — during lunch break at a conference or training session, for example.

STEP 1

Distribute paper and pencils to everyone present with the instructions that each person is to write out the 50 states in alphabetical order, spelled correctly. Then collect the sheets and allow a few moments to pass (during which the facilitator should pretend to be "grading" the quizzes).

STEP 2

Arrange everyone into three groups — one very small group (that will represent the wealthy); one about twice that size (that will represent the middle class) and one including the majority of those present (representing the masses of poor people or so-called "third world" nations). It will generally be assumed that these groups were selected based on achievement scores on the 50 states quiz — in actuality, they may be selected at random.

STEP 3

Distribute boxes of food to each group. The smallest, elite group representing the wealthy receives more than enough food — in fact, enough food to feed everyone in the room adequately. The middle group receives just enough food to feed their group. And the largest group receives only an onion and a small container of mustard.

STEP 4

Allow the groups to eat and wait to see what happens. If possible, the facilitator can arrange the room so that the wealthy group also has nicely decorated tables; the middle group has adequate seating but only the basics; and "the masses" must sit on the floor a substantial distance from everyone else.

"*It was obvious to us, okay, here they are testing us, we've learned all these things, so we tried to cooperate. And that was really interesting because we couldn't cooperate. It was really hard.*"

— Vanderbilt University student

PROCESSING

Following the simulation, time should be allotted for processing and discussion, both in the small groups and with the rest of the people in the room.

"And the group that had the most lorded it over them and gave them and gave them a sort of nobles oblige idea — okay, here... They made it sound like, 'You can have this sandwich and you can have this brownie, aren't we nice?' They didn't say that, but it was definitely the spirit of what happened. And the middle class just said, 'Well, let's share our excess, but we'll take care of ourselves first."

— Vanderbilt University student

SOURCE:
Vanderbilt student, originally developed by Diane Hedin

"The Watch" — Beginning the Process of Critical Reflection

This provides students with a shared experience exposing our failures of observation and forcing the mind to begin using critical reflection skills. Use to introduce students to concept of critical reflection and then move to apply critical reflection techniques to their service.

PURPOSE:

◆

Reframing

PROCESS

Warm-up exercise

STEP 1

Ask students to draw their watch faces in detail without looking at them.

STEP 2

Each student than shows drawing to a partner, and they compare with actual watch. Most will find that they don't know what their watch looks like although they have looked at it thousands of times.

STEP 3

Explore with students reasons why this phenomenon occurs.

- ◆ What assumptions have they made about watches?

- ◆ Why has frequent observation not corrected their assumptions?

Introduce the concept of *critical reflection* — the need to question fundamental assumptions.

SAMPLE QUESTIONS TO LINK EXERCISE TO CRITICAL REFLECTION ABOUT SERVICE:

- ◆ How do our assumptions about things affect what we observe?

- ◆ Can you think of examples of how your assumptions have shaped how you see things?

- ◆ What assumptions have you made about the people and places where we are performing community service?

- ◆ What assumptions have you made about the causes of the community problems we are involved with?

- ◆ What have you observed that fits these assumptions?

- Are there things you have observed that don't fit these assumptions?

- Are there other ways to view these people, places and problems?

- What information would you need to test your assumptions?

VARIATIONS

There are dozens of exercises — frequently found in psychology texts — in which people's perceptions of a visual stimulus, or of a task is shaped by context or by previous assumptions. They are often found in lists of 'brain teasers' or puzzles. Any of these exercises can be used to explore how unexamined assumptions are a barrier to understanding and solving social problems. The key is to explore the phenomenon with a simple puzzle or exercise and then to move the idea of questioning assumptions to the issues and experiences of the service-learning.

Another Exercise

TASK

Arrange the glasses so that the filled and empy ones alternate by touching or moving only one of the glasses. [coloring water with food coloring makes it more visually appealing]

FIRST ROUND   ### SOLUTION

Make a big show of moving the glasses into the pattern while describing the task.
Glasses are arranged as follows: Move glass **1**   Beside glass **5**

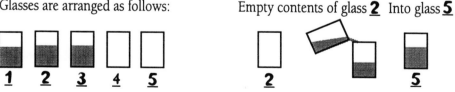

SECOND ROUND   ### SOLUTION

Now ask students to arrange the glasses in alternating pattern again; stress that only one glass may be moved.
Glasses are arranged as follows: Empty contents of glass **2** Into glass **5**

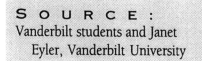

The first round fixes the view that the solution is to be found in moving glasses; the solution to the second problem is in moving the contents. Our assumptions about a problem sometimes reinforced by previous experience may block understanding and effective solutions to new problems.

S O U R C E :
Vanderbilt students and Janet
Eyler, Vanderbilt University

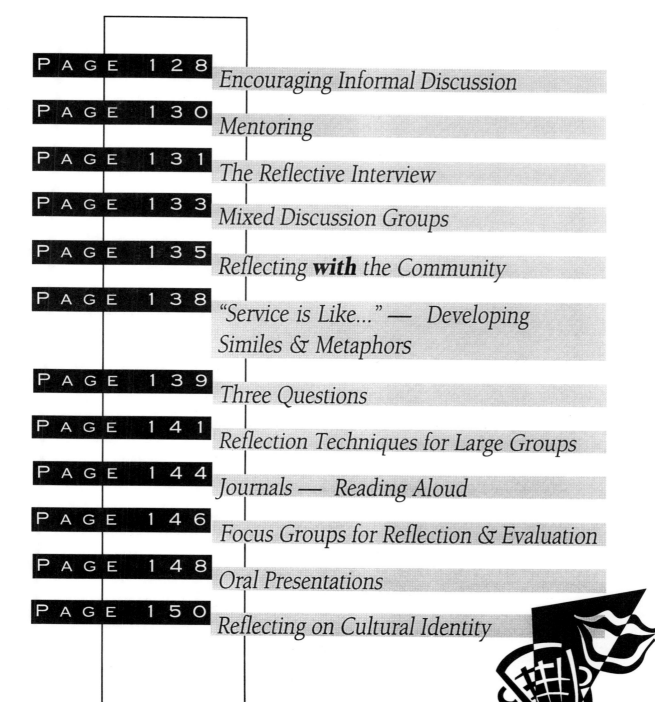

TELLING

Encouraging Informal Discussion

Many community service experiences occur without a classroom connection. And much useful reflection is informal, occurring with roommates, family and friends or with other volunteers 'in the van' on the way back from a site. Students may resist formal school-like assignments; faculty and program directors may want to encourage discussion designed to help students place their experience in a wider context.

"[The best reflection is]... just talking. Talking to my panel members, talking to my friends. I have one good friend, we have similar classes and we talk about the experiences and if I need help on a theory or something and I say, 'Where's an example of this?' She'll tell me, 'This is it.' And so, just a lot of verbal reflection is good."

— University of San Diego student

PROCESS

The key to encouraging reflection in non-classroom based community service activities is to build it into the natural flow of the experience, and informal reflection is a bonus for courses where structured reflection also occurs. Here are some methods to help in either scenario:

Team Leaders as Facilitators

Set the expectation that team leaders will have responsibility for debriefing the service experience as well as for logistics. Provide these leaders with simple ideas for stimulating focused conversation 'in the van' or at other times the service-learners are together. For example: The leader can share an experience or a problem he or she had that day and invite sharing of similar experiences or suggestions for coping with the problem. The leader can establish 'van time' as problem solving time and have different students pose issues or concerns for feedback from other volunteers. The leader can encourage conversation by asking students to describe what they are doing, what surprises the day held, why they think the situations they are describing are occurring and what they think should be done about it. Encourage students to think beyond the specifics of the site to the broader social context of the problem they are dealing with.

PURPOSE:

◆

Personal Development

◆

*Connecting
with Others*

Buddy System

Establish a 'buddy system' where students volunteering in a setting are encouraged to discuss problems and issues with a particular fellow volunteer on a continuing basis.

Structuring the Site Assignment

Assigning volunteers to sites where they will work with staff and with other volunteers as well as work directly with community members will increase opportunities for informal discussion and reflection. This can be encouraged during training, by suggesting regular meetings with site personnel to discuss issues that arise. The quality of discussion will be higher if care is given to developing service opportunities that involve students in planning service with community members as well as delivering service.

Bring a Friend

Encourage volunteers to bring a friend for particular service activities. For example, tutors might bring friends to help with a party for the children at the school; coaches might bring friends to assist with a tournament; students working with the homeless might bring a friend to help serve at a holiday dinner; students with Habitat for Humanity might bring a roommate to help with construction. In the process of recruiting for a service activity, participants will need to discuss their service and its meaning with their friends.

"I actually — I took my roommate to my place of service because no one can understand what I feel when I leave there. It's not like a material thing that they give you. It's just sitting down with a bunch of girls. I knew I was once very lucky, I had older sisters. A lot of them don't have older sisters to talk to. And I took my roommate and she understood. I think when other people come with you they understand the feelings that you have when you leave."   — University of Washington student

Adding Reflection to 'Logistics' Meetings

Establish regular meeting times for the students and use that time to help them identify and solve 'nuts and bolts' problems they are having with their service tasks. In the course of these site oriented problem solving sessions, the discussion can also be directed to placing problems in a broader context. Discussions, for example, of better ways to work with children who are being tutored can also include discussion of why these children are having difficulty and what the community might do to prevent the problems that give rise to need for service. The practical problems serve as a platform for addressing more complex issues.

> **SOURCE**
> Virtually every student from every school mentioned the importance of discussions with friends and family.

Mentoring

PURPOSE:

◆

Personal Development

◆

*Connecting
with Others*

◆

Understanding

Some service-learning programs establish mentoring pairs or teams within classes to encourage reflection. This is particularly useful when very large classes are involved, or where only some students are involved in service.

"Right now we're meeting every day because our assignment is due on Thursday. But, we try to talk at least once or twice a week. If not in class, then outside of class. And usually our experiences are different. So one person might be... in the third stage, and one person might have only gotten to the first stage. So, it's like a show and tell. I say, okay I have this experience and then someone will say, we did this and this is my experience. So we can each see how far the theory has gone with each person." — Bentley College student

PROCESS

STEP 1

Establish mentoring pairs or small teams of 3 or 4 students. Teams may be responsible for a team project such as a class presentation. Or mentors may be tasked with helping each other on the development of their individual papers or presentations.

STEP 2

Guide the teams through the mentoring process during one class or meeting session. Establish topics or tasks for mentors to assist with, and model the process. Have students practice with feedback from other teams or team members.

STEP 3

Have teams establish times to meet outside of class to assist each other.

SOURCE:
Bentley Students

The Reflective Interview
USING INDIVIDUAL INTERVIEWS TO REFLECT ON SERVICE-LEARNING EXPERIENCES

The basis for this guide is a set of personal interviews with over 60 college and university students from eight service-learning programs across the country. We designed this interview to be used for reflection as well as for its primary purpose in gathering research data. Our experience suggests that it can be modified and adapted in several ways to provide a tool for reflection. An Interview Guide is included in Appendix D, for readers who might be interested in our methodology or seeking examples to duplicate.

THE BENEFITS

One type of feedback we received from the students and program people involved was that the interview was user-friendly. This is evidenced by the fact that we had just under a 90% interview rate of students who agreed to do the interviews. This contrasts with our experience in using pencil and paper surveys, where we experienced about a 67% completion rate.

The major positive element of using the interview as a reflection tool as well as a research tool is that it helped students reflect across a longer time span than just one course or program experience. One student remarked that it helped him develop a "big picture" view of his involvement in service-learning courses.

PURPOSE:

Personal Development

◆

Understanding

PROCESS
STEP 1

We selected mostly students who had extensive service involvements and then sampled for both those who had high levels of reflective experiences and those who had fewer. In all cases students wrote a chronological list of their service involvements that the interviewer referred to in the interview. (See Interview Guide — Appendix D.)

STEP 2

The interviews generally lasted anywhere from 50 minutes to over an hour and were tape recorded and transcribed. There were three phases of the interview: a history of service; a recounting of what learning had occurred in these experiences and why; a section of "reflecting on reflection;" and a summary. It is from this last section that we are assembling the best practices of reflection as experienced by the students whom we interviewed.

Alternative Uses
for the Interview

◆ Exit interviews with graduating seniors to help them synthesize a big picture view of multiple service-learning involvements.

◆ Have students interview each other, using any or all of the five sections of the interview guide.

◆ Adapt the questions for a focus group.

◆ Use the interviews, especially the second section, as a way to assess and document student learning outcomes for both individual learning and program evaluation.

USING THE INTERVIEW

We used questions from this interview in reflection workshops with Corporation for National Service (CNS) grantees to identify their experiences in designing reflection activities. The interview can be adapted to meet the needs of any number of individuals and circumstances, a few of which are noted in this page's Sidebar listing.

However the interview is modified or used, several elements seem crucial:

◆ The chance to stop and verbalize one's reflections

◆ The presence of a sympathetic listener as an interviewer

◆ The assistance of the prompts and probes to develop a full picture of service-learning experiences and their meanings

VARIATION
Interviewing Community Members

Students can construct interview protocols and interview people working in the community. (See Oral Histories on Page 110 for a similar project)

"The first semester of my sophomore year, we had to interview a black educator, there was something that was incorporated into the service learning. But, it's like you still were — we were required to make a presentation, and oral presentation for our class." — Clark Atlanta University student

S O U R C E :
Janet Eyler & Dwight Giles, Vanderbilt University; Clark Atlanta University and East Tennessee State University students

Mixed Discussion Groups

WHEN ONLY SOME CLASS MEMBERS ARE DOING SERVICE-LEARNING

Instructors and students sometimes find it awkward to integrate service experiences of students into class when only some of the students are involved in service. With a little planning the necessary continuity can be established for service-learning students and the rest of the class can benefit as well.

PROCESS
STEP 1

Form discussion groups of about 6 students, half of whom are in service placements and half of whom are doing alternate research assignments.

PURPOSE:

◆

Connecting with Others

◆

Understanding

"She had us together, the research people and the service people. And then we were supposed to bring out common themes from both of our work and bring out something we learned that we all learned. For our group it was really easy... since we'd identified early what our goals were and what our themes were... Our group talked about poverty and homelessness and political strategies. The service people talked about how welfare was actually affecting people's lives... real specific stories... And those doing research would bring in the numbers and the data. You still got the feeling in the research of people's lives being disrupted in a different way than what the policy was maybe aiming for. But you don't get a good understanding of that until you talk to somebody who has a name." — University of Washington student

STEP 2

Periodically ask the teams to meet during class to discuss targeted topics. The service students are specifically charged to share relevant observations from their service experience and the others to share results of their library research. For example: some students can discuss the literature on tracking while their service-learning counterparts share examples of the impact of tracking on the students they are tutoring; some can provide information on environmental policy while others can provide details about the implementation of recycling, or water quality efforts they are observing in the field; some can provide information on welfare reform proposals while others provide insights from working with families in homeless shelters or in emergency food programs. Groups may be asked to share key insights with the entire class.

"The people who didn't do the service would spend as much time in the library as I would in the soup kitchen. ...Both of us really had thought a lot about the issue... and so they knew what they were talking about but they really didn't feel what they were talking about kind of... I think they were probably as committed to it as I was but it just never got expressed."
— East Tennessee State University student

SOURCE:
University of Washington and
Eastern Tennessee State
University Students

Reflecting **with** the Community

It was unusual for students to mention reflection sessions with community members, but those who did found them to be very powerful, especially in helping them understand perspectives they hadn't thought of before.

PROCESS

The key to creating reflection sessions that include community members is in the design of the student placement. Where students are working with community members to plan projects, or are in situations where debriefings are part of the culture of the organization opportunities for community based reflection are built in. It is also possible to create these opportunities by inviting community members to class or creating reflection sessions at the site.

"I went to a conference of the student coalition for action in literacy education and they had different... workshops you could attend. And one was for the new readers. They had about one fifth of the participants in the conference were new readers and it was very interesting to interact with these people and to hear what they thought. And they came up with things that the students hadn't thought of such as choosing reading materials and why these reading materials are inaccessible, but these aren't and things like that. These are the people who are leading the lives that we're trying to help and it doesn't make sense to me to exclude them from the decision-making."

— University of Washington student

PURPOSE:

◆

Connecting with Others

◆

Understanding

◆

Reframing

VARIATIONS

Routine Organizational Debriefings

Some community service organizations routinely schedule sessions to discuss incidents or to debrief participants about ongoing issues. For example: emergency rescue squads may meet and review difficult rescue situations; hot lines may periodically hold sessions to discuss procedure and coping with difficult situations; agencies may periodically analyze breakdowns in services provided to community members. When establishing the service-learning site, the instructor or coordinator should find out about these procedures and arrange for student participants to be included in this "real world" reflection.

"After a real bad incident has occurred... he'll call the debriefing team... And then all the agencies that were there and all the personnel that were there on the scene... meet... We'll sit in a circle. Heads of the departments will sit with their own members... it's more or less to relieve the frustration, relieve the strain. Just talk about it and — let people know that nothing there was their fault. Everybody there did the best they could — and if somebody dies, we try to get over it. There's always heated discussions. Like funding is a big one and not using the resources adequately... like when the car was hit by the train and one of the victims — her body was in view of the bystanders... there were three or four coroners there on the scene that could have got her body out of there, but because of politics, they've got this coroner's list and they start at the top of the list... the guy at the top of the list... there was some time for him to get there... they had to wait for this one person because of politics. That was brought out — there were three or four on the scene who could have her on the way. They had to wait for that one person." — Eastern Tennessee State University student

"I think the main thing that helps is that all of us in the organization, we sit down and talk about the different problems — and also, you can't find the solutions to problems in books, you can get a basic understanding, maybe — but until you deal with the problem and have to focus on it, you don't know how to respond to that. So a lot of times it helps to sit down in a group. We do it every Sunday... We've had parent attacks in the last year and I think I was the first person who learned how to deal with it. Then I talked to other mentors about it — and it's like one of his kids, his mother attacked him and he had to talk about it and deal with it... and I talked to him about how I dealt with it. We meet Sundays for 4 or 5 hours."

— Clark Atlanta University student

Reflection Sessions with Agency Constituents

Invite agency personnel and the community members they work with, to meet with students to discuss issues that arise in the field. This is an important part of orientation sessions for students, but may be even more useful later in the service semester when students are concerned about specific tasks, problems or issues. Discussion can be structured around the ways in which various participants define the problem that the service addresses or around changes that should be made in the way service is provided or in public policy.

Community members can also be included in class discussions, if the invitation would be appropriate given the context of the relationship.

Projects with Community Members

Where projects are designed to include community members and students in the planning process, opportunities for reflection are built into the experience.

"...Lots of community interaction... When setting up the program, you have a committee, you have a few of [the community agency constituents] on the committee. That, to me, is very important - just having all sides represented in the decision-making - whatever the decision-making may be. Maybe with Habitat having a few home owners on the campus board working with the students saying, 'well this is what I feel they should be educated about, so why don't you do this during homeless awareness week?'— and having that input. I think it really crashes the ego sometimes of students who are leading it or whoever the leaders are that they can't feel like they know everything."

— Vanderbilt University student

SOURCE:
Eastern Tennessee State
    University, Clark Atlanta and
    Vanderbilt students

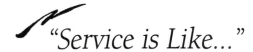

"Service is Like..."
DEVELOPING SIMILES AND METAPHORS

Constructing a metaphor, simile or analogy for their service experience helps students analyze its meaning.

PROCESS

This technique can be used as a warm up exercise for a large group or as a wrap-up or summary exercise.

PURPOSE:

◆

Understanding

STEP 1

Provide an example of a metaphor that illustrates the meaning of the service-learning experience. These can be obtained from past students, developed by the facilitator, or drawn from the student comment at the bottom of this page.

STEP 2

Ask student teams to construct a metaphor that captures the essence of their service-learning experience.

Or ask students to respond to the prompt:

My service this semester is like _____

because _____

Students then share and discuss their similes or metaphors with the class.

"*My analogy is — the class is like a piece of paper and then being able to do the community service, it animates that picture. So, you have a piece of paper with maybe a cartoon on it, and you can read the cartoon and understand the cartoon, but when you do the community service it animates the cartoon and turns the cartoon piece of paper into an actual movie and then you can experience the movie and maybe even you're a part of the movie. So it's like the class is the piece of paper and the community service brings it to life and makes sense of why you're even there.*" — University of San Diego student

SOURCE:
Students at University of San Diego and University of Washington

Three Questions

Like the writing strategies discussed in Applying Kolb's Model (See page 97), "Three Questions" provides a structure for debriefing field experiences that can be used repeatedly; if used consistently students quickly adopt the structure, and the quality of their observations and analysis improves. As students spend more time in the field emphasis will be placed on application.

PROCESS

Students consistently praised discussion techniques that pushed them beyond simple sharing. In fact many students complained about discussions that simply involved expressing feelings or recounting the days events. One version presented focused discussion around three types of questions:

- What did you see?

- How did you feel about it?

- How can you apply it?

Structuring discussion around these explicit 'steps' left students feeling that the reflection sessions were purposive and not just aimless — and sometimes boring — re-tellings of experience.

THE KEY TO THIS APPROACH

The key to the effectiveness of this simple approach was that the questions and steps were made very explicit and followed repeatedly. During the descriptive phase no feelings or opinions were to be shared. Great attention was paid to describing things as accurately as possible without interpretation. Once attention had been focused on describing the experience, interpretation became more fruitful. And this made application easier. Types of application included:

- Linking experiences to class readings or theories

- Proposing solutions to social problems

- Planning community action.

"There's three stages to it... the first one was just the person's observations — this was really difficult for a lot of people because it was not just your feelings about it. It was just observations. For example, juvenile hall — 'what did you see?' — well we went in there and there were a lot of gangs and it — no feelings — just senses basically. Just the real

PURPOSE:

◆

Understanding

◆

Application

nuts and bolts. Just what you observed without anything attached to that. That was the first part. It was difficult, but I think it was necessary to just split that apart — because so commonly, people put those two together — what they observed and their feelings and to come up with something in the middle. And to separate them is difficult. But it aids in introspection and understanding. And the next one feelings are involved... how you felt about certain things... the last one was kind of an analysis of the experience and how it applied to something. It was very structured and it separated observations from feelings from just an overall analysis... I really liked that reflection."

— University of San Diego student

VARIATIONS

The *"What? So What? Now What?"* discussion method based on Kolb's model and introduced in Chapter 1 (See Page 16) is a similar approach that was mentioned as useful.

SOURCE:
University of San Diego and
Vanderbilt University students

Reflection Techniques for Large Group Discussion

Formal discussions with service-learners are often difficult because students sometimes resist 'classroom-like' assignments and activities when they participate in a co-curricular service-learning effort. Techniques which involve activity are more likely to engage students; the same techniques can be used to vary discussions in the classroom as well.

PROCESS

These three pages provide several examples suggested by students and Learn and Serve Program Directors.

Ball Toss

A useful way to encourage active participation yet maintain control is for the facilitator at a retreat or other large meeting to throw a tennis ball to an individual who then has the floor. When this person is finished he or she than tosses the ball back to the facilitator who throws it to another person. The ball can also be tossed from participant to participant. It is an especially useful technique for brainstorming or quick sharing of multiple anecdotes.

Yarn Web

This is a similar technique where students seated in a circle toss a ball of yarn to each other as they share ideas or experiences. The yarn creates a web as it unravels and this becomes an object lesson for further reflection The web represents the interconnectedness of people and their experiences.

Post It Notes

Post-it Notes are a convenient way to encourage active participation in sharing ideas or reactions. They may be used to create Likert scale displays where students paste up their notes from strongly agree to strongly disagree and create a visual distribution. Or they may be used to write questions or comments and pasted to appropriate posters. Or they may be used to evaluate an experience, allowing anonymous though immediate feedback. A special advantage of using notes for these various purposes is that all participants can observe and read reactions of their peers.

PURPOSE:
◆
Multiple Purposes

What Do We Want to Know?

At the beginning of a meeting or retreat, students can be encouraged to list questions on sheets of paper posted at the room entrance. These questions then can serve as the jumping off place for group discussion. Note cards can also be used to assemble questions. This allows the facilitator to structure the flow of questions while responding to the concerns of the group.

Giant Likert Scale

Creating a giant Likert type scale on the walls of a room is a dramatic way to engage students in a discussion of their different perspectives and also to introduce information about community service issues. Five signs — **Strongly Agree, Agree, Undecided, Disagree** and **Strongly Disagree** are placed around a room much as they would be on a questionnaire. Target questions are read and students group themselves according to their position on the items. After about half a dozen items, students are ready to sit down and explore the issues raised by the exercise.

"We put pieces of paper on the floor with strongly agree and strongly disagree and... flew out statements... some very bland... some very poignant, specific and biased. And then had them react to it and put themselves — physically move on the continuum. We started out with some issues [related to our service] like '80% of old people can't take care of themselves'... and then we had some other ones that were kind of related to just training and quality service... like 'people who are only doing service so they can put it on their resumes shouldn't do it.' or stuff like 'it is absolutely important for those who are serving to get as much out of the experience as those who are served.' We did it in a way that tried to get them riled up... that was the whole point of the biased statements... they were asked to sit down or if they had a comment to remain standing... we had a lot of disagreements and some of them we didn't call on... and they got so frustrated and they're like "what I believe is important" and so then, we'd reach a critical mass and break into smaller groups and this wonderful discussion came out of that... I'm always happy to see passion in discussion." — Vanderbilt University student

Reflection Stations

Large sheets of paper headed by target questions for reflection can be posted. Students can move about and respond to questions that interest them. Examples include:

- ◆ What has been your biggest surprise during your service?

- What was your most memorable experience?

- What do you feel best about?

- What disturbs or puzzles you?

- How has your service changed the way you think?

Participants can view the questions posted by their peers and facilitators can synthesize the results and use them to begin broader group discussion.

Table Team Reports

Large groups which include students in diverse service settings can begin discussion by grouping students in table teams around common experiences, issues or themes. For example, tables could be labeled with the type of service e.g. homelessness, food programs, tutoring or the environment. Students with common experiences would then work together to develop a presentation for the group in response to stem questions. For example:

- What were your most memorable experiences?

- How did the way you think about the people and the issue you worked with change?

- What were your biggest disappointments and of what were you proudest?

- If you were designing programs for the people you have worked with, what would you do differently?

The same technique could be used with students from very different service placements. Teams might explore how particular situations were similar and different.

Table Team Posters

Instead of orally presenting the results of their discussion, table teams can also be asked to create a poster illustrating their main points. Posters can be taped to walls and in very large groups where oral presentations might be too time consuming, students can move about the room reading the work of other teams. Using the walls as a scrapbook for displaying work that students have done during their service can be an effective way to share student efforts and to make individual work public.

Three Generalizations and a Question

Ask small groups of students to create three generalizations about their target issue or topic based on their service experience and one question they would like to have answered. These can be listed on butcher paper and posted and presented to the group.

SOURCE:
Source: students from several schools, Learn and Serve Directors at summer workshops, Vanderbilt service-learning programs.

Journaling
READING ALOUD

When students know they may be called to read from their journals as a way to begin class discussions, they may be motivated to complete their journals regularly and to put more thought into their writing. It may be a particularly useful technique to use with students who are not comfortable with writing; the public reading reinforces their efforts, and some students may find writing easier when they think of it as a prelude to oral expression.

The public questioning helps model the kinds of inquiry that the teacher would like to encourage in future journals.

PURPOSE:

◆

Multiple Purposes

"*We seldom get through a whole report because he fires questions at us... he wants to stimulate us to think about all facets of the internships than perhaps we otherwise would.*

...And the whole class benefits because you may not even be called on during a particular week, but you hear the types of questions that were asked this week and you say, 'I better make sure that I make this type of observation or incorporate this into my reflection next week.'"

— Clark Atlanta University student

PROCESS

This journal technique moves the experience from a personal to a public record; the written record becomes the focal point of an oral group activity.

STEP 1

Students are asked to keep journals of their field experiences. They are directed to both describe what they see and do and to provide their own interpretative comments. In co-curricular settings, this process may take place during a group meeting — the facilitator simply gathers the group together for instructions and topic assignments; the group disperses for long enough to write alone, and then reconvenes for the remainder of the activity.

STEP 2

During each class (or whenever the whole group is able to reconvene), students are asked to read passages from their journals to initiate debriefing sessions on service experience.

They may read about what they did and observed or may read their analysis of and emotional reactions to their experience.

STEP 3

The facilitator then directs questions to the student whose work has been read. The questions are designed to elicit further information and to push the student to interpret and apply the experience. These questions push the current discussion, but also model the kinds of questions that students might ask themselves as they write their next journal entries. For sample questions, see Critical Questions (Page 95), in the Writing section of this chapter.

STEP 4

Other students are then encouraged to contribute related observations or insights. They may either comment on journal entries already read or contribute some material from their own journal entries.

Students found the experience useful as a way to focus the discussion on something concrete i.e. a particular students experience and also useful in pushing them to think and write about their service experiences with greater depth.

S O U R C E :

Students from Clark Atlanta University

Focus Groups for Reflection and Evaluation

PURPOSE:

Connecting to Others
◆
Understanding

Although focus groups are traditionally used in marketing research, several opportunities exist for their use in service-learning. Practitioners can use focus groups to encourage reflection by structuring dialogue among students. Focus groups are also a qualitative methodology useful for formative and summative evaluations of outcomes from a service-learning experience.

PROCESS

Focus groups are generally composed of a moderator or facilitator trained in group dynamics and 4-12 participants who have common characteristics, e.g., students currently involved in community service. By using a set of focused yet open-ended questions, focus group moderators can cultivate self-discovery. This technique is based on the Socratic method of instruction. The moderator asks a set of structured questions that move from general to more specific, allowing him or her to probe responses if necessary. There are both advantages and disadvantages to using focus groups as reflection and/or assessment tools.

Advantages

- ◆ Participants learn from others' insights and perspectives

- ◆ Instructor can achieve economy of scale through group versus individual reflection

- ◆ Moderator can probe participants' responses for clarity and elaboration

- ◆ Session can be recorded, analyzed and used for assessment purposes

Disadvantages

- ◆ If used for evaluation purposes, students in a course may give "desirable" rather than candid responses

- ◆ Not all participants may contribute equally

- ◆ Evaluation data are costly to transcribe and difficult to analyze

STEP 1

Establish a set of structured questions before conducting the interview. Link questions to specific outcomes or objectives of your service-learning course or project (e.g., citizenship development, problem-solving ability). For sample questions, see the sidebar listing on the facing page.

STEP 2

At the beginning of the session, state that you are interested in everyone's views. Throughout the discussion, continue to encourage multiple perspectives.

STEP 3

Ensure that the moderator understands group processes:

◆ Minimize dominance from "excessive talkers" by focusing eye contact on other participants

◆ Involve non-talkers by directly questioning them

◆ Encourage candid dialogue by avoiding affirmative/negative verbal and nonverbal responses (e.g., frowning, excessive head nodding).

If you have concerns about equal participation from students, use the nominal group technique of having students write their individual responses to questions and then discussing them as a group. It is useful to collect these responses for assessment purposes as well.

STEP 5

When questioning, use probes such as:

◆ "Say more about that."

◆ "Can you give me an example?"

◆ "Does anyone have a different point of view on that subject?"

S O U R C E :
Students from Vanderbilt University; Angela Schmiede, Vanderbilt University

SAMPLE QUESTIONS FOR FOCUS GROUPS

◆

"We are interested in your views about how important problems in our society should be solved. What are some of the issues you have observed or heard about in your community service experiences?"

◆

"How would you describe this problem?"

◆

"What are some things that come to mind when confronted with this problem?"

◆

"What has caused this problem?"

◆

"What are some possible solutions to this problem? Can you think of anything else to do?"

◆

"What steps would have to be taken to implement your solution(s)?"

◆

"If you wanted to get personally involved in solving this problem in your community, what would you do?"

◆

"What have you learned from your service that makes you a more effective participant in the community?"

◆

"Are there some "rules of thumb" or guidelines for community involvement that you think people should know in order to be effective in community action? What skills or knowledge are necessary to be effective?"

Reflection Activities • Chapter 4

Oral Presentations

By using the service experience as a case study to illustrate a theory being developed in class, students are able to anchor their understanding in their concrete experience. This activity closely resembles the "Theory into Practice" option described in the Student Facilitation exercise (Page 102).

PURPOSE:

◆

Understanding

◆

Application

"*We also had to do the presentation at the end. All the people that worked at the shelter, it was about 12 of us — the shelter I worked at, it was set up for different nights and we'd go a certain night each week. There were about 4 who went my week. We had to meet and present our project. Who we worked with and talk about how — it was kind of like the journal, but we had to — we had to talk more about the sociological perspective. And that presentation made us focus even more.*" — University of Washington student

PROCESS
STEP 1

Teams of students are asked to choose events they have observed in their service setting and use them to illustrate concepts or theories being developed in the service-learning class.

STEP 2

Each team then presents their case to the class in the form of some sort of oral presentation such as speeches, slide shows or multimedia presentations. Students have the experience of seeing if the theories help illuminate their own experience, and they have the opportunity to hear other concrete applications.

LEARNING FROM FAILURE

The student who shared this technique was involved in a failed project with a residence for people with AIDS. In spite of numerous attempts to get the group and the directors of the residence together to plan a service activity, and several meetings between team members and residents nothing much was accomplished.

This frustrating experience from a service perspective became a learning experience through application of this assignment. The students used theories related to communications failure and found that the failure to connect made sense in terms of these theories. So while frustrated at one level, they were able to contribute case examples to their peers who were explaining their successes with other theoretical perspectives.

VARIATIONS

Students Provide Service Examples

When theories and concepts are being introduced in lecture and class discussion students who are participating in service can be asked to share examples from their experience. This can be a very effective way for a class to benefit from the experiences of those who have selected the service option in a class where many students are doing other assignments.

Student Panels

Students involved in community service can present panels within the larger class. These may be largely descriptive or may involve students in the preparation of organizational or problem analysis presentations linked to the curriculum.

"*I have had to interview social workers or go to social service agencies in an event. Come back and address the class on what I observed, the surroundings and then what they told me. How they perceived it. How I perceived it. If that was different and why. Each student took a different agency, so we were in charge of coming back and telling them all about that agency or at least what we could find out.*"

— East Tennessee State University student

Community Presentations

Students may develop public presentations about their service-learning experience for delivery to other students within the college or university or for community groups.

Other Presentations

Most of the projects and activities described in the Writing and Doing sections of this guide can serve as the basis of classroom or community presentations. For many students, providing an oral as well as a written component for their work motivates more thoughtful work.

SOURCE:

Students from all colleges

Reflecting on Cultural Identity

A number of students mentioned the impact that cultural and ethnic differences encountered through service-learning had on their thinking and awareness of social issues. This exercise attempts to isolate those issues for discussion and enhanced understanding.

PROCESS

PREPARATION

When preparing for this activity, a solid sense of trust among participants is crucial. It should be scheduled in conjunction with earlier group building strategies and after the group has established a solid base of shared experiences. Beginning the session with an opportunity for each individual to identify his or her own cultural heritage — this self-identification is a clarifying and empowering experience for most individuals

STEP 1

Students should start by forming groups based on common cultural identity. Try not to structure the formation of groups—remember that cultural identity is based on individual perceptions and can involve multiple factors. *Self*-identification should be the guiding philosophy in this exercise.

Groups can be any size, even as small as one if a person feels that his or her cultural identity is extremely different from others in the group. Some groups that may emerge include the following:

- ◆ White Jewish American Women
- ◆ African Americans
- ◆ Hispanic Men
- ◆ First Generation Born to European Immigrants
- ◆ Asian Americans raised in Southern U.S.

PURPOSE:

◆

Understanding

◆

Reframing

STEP 2

Once the groups have formed, give them 20 minutes to generate a list of stereotypes generally associated with their particular culture.

STEP 3

Each group will then create a presentation with the purpose of educating the rest of the group on something related to that culture. For example, groups do presentations on particular aspects of their culture. Students may choose to perform songs, dances, skits or poems, addressing any number of issues:

- History
- Geography
- Music
- Dance
- Religious customs

STEP 4

After each group presents to the larger group, allow time for a question and answer period. Then, to debrief the session, have students discuss or journal reflections about stereotypes the may have had about a particular culture and how these presentations have reframed the way they view a particular culture.

"*As far as reflecting, being able to reflect on what we've talked about. I haven't finished all my reflections. The ones I have finished, yes, it's definitely helped to think about race and ethnicity. This is what my class is. And then seeing the different races and ethnicities when I'm working with those people and stuff. So, relating the two. There's no major theories in this class — it's more just learning about different races and different ethnicities in society and how we're all affected by them.*" — University of San Diego student

S O U R C E :
Vanderbilt University student; and Posse Plus Retreat with the Vanderbilt Community, January 1996 (Posse Foundation, New York, NY).

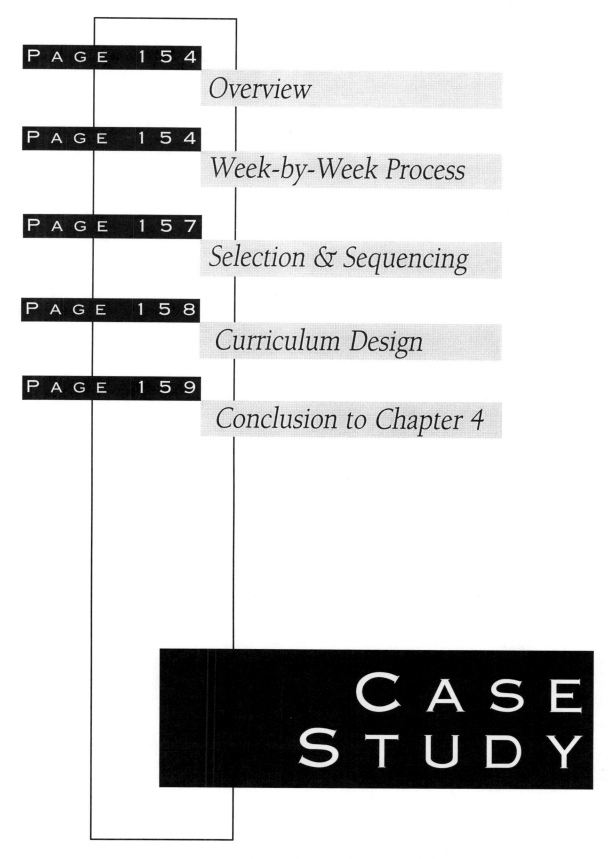

CASE STUDY

INTRODUCTION

The following case study is an example of how to structure and sequence a semester-long intensive field experience. The reflection activities cited in the case study are included in sample reflection activities that make up the four previous sections of this chapter. These activities provide a basic *framework* for designing an activity. The content and topic for each activity can easily be adapted to a particular service-learning course or project. For example, the journal reflection assignments on page 78 can just as easily be used in an educational policy course as a chemistry service-learning course. The structure trains students to reflect thoroughly on a particular event, regardless of the context.

Case Study

OVERVIEW

The 13 week service-learning internship consists of a 32 hour/week field experience which is integrated with a three hour weekly seminar. Each week in seminar, students have the opportunity to share, compare, and contrast experiences. This time is also used to problem-solve any issues related to service or their roles as interns. These sessions vary in terms of structure and leadership by a faculty facilitator.

WEEK 1

◆ Students are asked to write an "Ideal Letter of Recommendation" (see page 85) which they would like to receive from their supervisor at the end of the term. In the letter, students cite goals they have met, competencies they have achieved and tangible products they have created for the organization. The letter encourages students to think about goals they would like to develop for their internships. The students are then assigned to read portions of Malcolm Knowles' *Using Learning Contracts* (1986) to provide a theoretical foundation in goal-setting.

◆ Students are assigned to read Suezle and Borzak's "Stages of Fieldwork" (1981) to provide a conceptual framework for specified developmental tasks for each stage of the internship.

◆ Students are assigned to read a portion of Bolman and Deal's *Reframing Organizations: Artistry, Choice, and Leadership* (1991) to prepare them for several organizational analysis assignments. These readings and assignments are designed to give students a better understanding of how their organization functions internally and externally.

WEEK 2

◆ Students begin a series of weekly presentations on their organization over the next four weeks. The presentation topics become progressively more complex and abstract as interns assimilate more knowledge about their organizations over time. This week they give a 5 minute presentation on their organization from a structural perspective. This exercise serves several purposes: to introduce the use of inquiry and observation skills; to practice presentation skills; and, to apply concepts from assigned readings to their on-site experience.

◆ Students take *Kolb's Learning Style Inventory* (McBer and Co. 1976) in class to assess their preferred learning style. This exercise provides a rationale for experiential education and allows students to identify weaknesses and strengths and develop goals in expanding learning styles.

◆ Students are assigned a draft learning plan with stated goals, activities and evidence of goal achievement during the internship.

WEEK 3

◆ Students give a 5 minute presentation of their organization from a human resource perspective.

◆ Students are assigned a "First Impressions" Reflection Assignment. This assignment requires that students use observation skills and field notes to reflect on and analyze their entry into the organization. Assigned readings are applied and integrated with the student's experience. This assignment is revisited at the end of the term.

WEEK 4

◆ Students give a 5 minute presentation of their organization from a symbolic or cultural perspective.

◆ Students are encouraged to move from a concrete and descriptive understanding of their organizations to a more integrated and analytic understanding of their organizations through an assigned "Organizational Analysis Paper" (see page 91) .

WEEK 5

◆ Students give a 5 minute presentation of their organization from a political perspective.

◆ Using their organizational analysis, students identity an organizational, community, or social problem related to their internship site. To gain a clearer understanding of this problem and identify solutions, they conduct library and field research. Students provide a brief analysis of the problem and propose a feasible solution to their supervisor in the form of a memo (see page 85).

WEEK 6

◆ Students conduct a midterm assessment of their goals, analyze feedback received from supervisor during a performance evaluation, and update their learning plans for the remainder of the term. In addition, students analyze progress achieved thus far by presenting portfolio (See page 82) items of work they have produced to meet learning goals. This entire process challenges students to reflect on their goals, activities, and accomplishments.

WEEK 7

◆   Students begin individualized readings and research to become "experts" on the problem analyzed in Week 5. Students use a variety of methods (literature review, interviews, survey research, etc.) to gather information about the issue they are analyzing. The issue is analyzed in the form of a project analysis paper. Students interviewed for this guide analyzed issues such as teenage alcohol abuse and restructuring of a national service organization and developed solutions to these problems into projects.

◆   Students analyze, compare, and contrast their stage of development in their field experience through oral discussion. This discussion usually involves the development of an action plan for those who have not progressed from the initiation stage to the competency stage.

WEEK 8

◆   Students meet individually with their faculty advisor to discuss their project. Faculty encourage students to reflect on the process by which they are creating their projects through dialogue.

◆   Students are assigned a reflection assignment which asks students to identify an external environment issue which relates to their organizations (See page 91). Students analyze these issues and integrate assigned readings about the external environment.

WEEK 9

◆   Faculty invite outside experts to serve as consultants to students during the seminar. The consultants serve as an additional resource to students as they complete their projects. They also encourage students to consider alternative perspectives in addressing these issues.

WEEK 10

◆   Students assess and reflect on their professional and decision making skills by participating in a series of simulations and assessment centers. An important part of these exercises is debriefing each activity and asking students to reflect on their performance.

WEEK 11

◆   Students meet individually with faculty advisors to discuss progress on completing project and compiling portfolio. These discussions usually include an analysis of goal achievement and an action plan for the remaining few weeks.

WEEK 12

◆   This week's seminar is used as a vehicle to prepare students to bring closure to their service experience. Students identify an action plan for bringing appropriate closure to their experience and discuss the final stage of fieldwork — Completion.

◆   Students present their portfolio of achievements and are asked to identify and explain their most significant accomplishment (see page 82). Students analyze their ability to meet learning plan goals in a final reflection assignment. In addition, the "Ideal Letter of Recommendation" is revisited in order to compare expected and achieved goals.

◆   Students complete a placement assessment paper which allows them to evaluate their placement in terms of a valuable learning experience. In this paper, students are encouraged to identify and articulate the types of learning goals which would be well suited to this type of placement.

◆   Students and faculty write letters to themselves (see page 85) following the "What?/ So What?/Now What?" model. Participants outline their one-year and five-year personal, professional, and educational goals. The letters are sealed, self-addressed and sent to each writer in three months. This exercise is useful in encouraging students to continue to evaluate and establish goals after the serving experience has ended.

WEEK 13

◆   The final week of the field experience allows students to demonstrate their ability to analyze, apply and integrate the learning which has occurred for them during the service-learning experience as well as earlier significant learning experiences. Students give a final project presentation which illustrates their abilities to synthesize information and present their projects in a persuasive manner.

The final project is evidence that transformation has occurred. The sidebar on page 158 displays sample projects completed by students.

SELECTION AND SEQUENCING

Assignments were sequenced to facilitate students' development throughout the field experience. This sequence is based on Suezle and Borzak's "Stages of Fieldwork" (1981). During the entry stage, it is important that students ask members in the organization questions. Students also need to be aware of using and developing observation skills. During the initiation stage, students should reflect on their socialization process. It is during this stage that students begin to clearly define their role and should begin setting specific goals for themselves.

During the competency stage, students need to engage in self-directed inquiry and generally become more autonomous in completing tasks and projects. It is important to develop specific areas of knowledge and skill during this time. The completion stage is an

SAMPLE PROJECTS COMPLETED BY STUDENTS:

Creation of a *Students Against Drunk Driving* (SADD) Program to be implemented in a local school.

A redesigned organizational chart accompanied by new and revised job descriptions for members of a national service organization.

A grant proposal to request funding for a youth development program.

opportunity to reflect on learning which has occurred as a result of the field experience. It is also a good time to reflect on long-term goals.

Reflection activities were selected to require use of a variety of learning styles. The activities included a combination of reading, writing, doing and telling. Similarly, the activities are structured so that students learn by feeling, watching, listening, thinking, and experimenting. Assignments begin on a more concrete level and gradually increase in complexity and synthesis. The ultimate goal of the seminar is to help students "reframe" how they view themselves, organizations, and social problems in the community.

CURRICULUM DESIGN

This service-learning internship program is a full-time capstone to a four year interdisciplinary program. The intensity and sequencing of reflection activities for any service-learning program will depend on a variety of factors, including the following:

- Students' prior service experience
- Level & amount of academic credit earned
- Frequency and duration of field experience
- Level of faculty involvement
- Number of participants
- Type of field experience

An effective sequence of activities will also incorporate the 4 C's that students identified as central to effective reflection. These elements were incorporated into the service-learning internship as follows:

1. *Continuous*

The curriculum is structured so that students continuously identify and analyze problems, identify appropriate solutions, implement ideas and solutions, and evaluate their effectiveness. By spending four days a week in the field and one day each week reflecting with faculty and peers on their experience the continuity of reflection is assured.

2. *Connected*

The assignments and activities relate to and build upon one another. Students are asked to use theories and models they have learned in their undergraduate courses and apply them to their field experiences. And their portfolio allows them to develop activities and structure reflections based on their learning goals.

3. *Challenging*

Perhaps the greatest challenge is that students were tasked with doing real work for real organizations. Students were constantly challenged to initiate change in their organizations. Their final project is a vehicle for impact. In addition, weekly structured reflection sessions allow faculty and students to provide feedback on projects as they develop. Much of the curriculum is self-directed so that students are challenged to take responsibility for their own learning and identify areas of inquiry relevant to their goals.

4. *Contextualized*

Service-learning interns spend four days a week in the field, and all their assignments asked them to work with experiences in the placement site. Students are immersed in the agency and experience the complexity of organizational life as they complete analyses and assessments of how their organization relates to the broader environment and their own particularized projects.

A FINAL NOTE ON CHAPTER 4

This chapter provides examples of dozens of reflection activities — any of which could be duplicated exactly to fill an immediate need — and a case study detailing one way in which some of the activities were combined and utilized effectively. It was never our intention, however, to supply a listing that would meet all of the needs of the service-learning practitioner. Rather, we have tried to pull from student interviewees' stories the sampling of activities that struck them as important for a number of reasons — for use as models that might be built upon and transformed in order to meet the needs of each reader.

The Introduction and Chapter 1, as well as the student commentary in Chapter 2, have provided some evidence for the importance of purposeful *Reflection* and have introduced *the 4 C's,* which will serve as basic guidelines as you work to develop innovative designs in reflection activities. Chapter 2 has also introduced the core outcomes of critical reflection as noted in the student interviews; and Chapter 3 has given some background on the other category that we use in the Reflection Activity Matrix on Page 65: Methodology

(Reading, Writing, Doing and Telling). By building on the theoretical and practical background provided in these previous chapter, you will be prepared and able to create and transform Chapter 4 reflection activities to meet the needs of your service-learning program.

FOR MORE INFORMATION

For additional information on the theoretical foundation and practical application of reflection in service-learning, we have included several bibliographies in the four appendices immediately following this chapter. Included in one is an annotated list of readings and similar materials that serve as excellent resources to accompany many of the reflection activities described in Chapter 4.

For readers who are interested in the research process used to develop this study, or for anyone hoping to use the reflection activity dealing with reflective interviews, we have also included a copy of the interview guide around which we structured the student interviews for this guide.

CHAPTER 4 REFERENCES

Bolman, L. & Deal, T. *Reframing Organizations: Artistry, Choice and Leadership.* San Francisco: Jossey-Bass, Inc., 1991

Daft, R.L. & Steers, R.M. *Organizations: A Micro/Macro Approach.* Glenview, IL: Scott Foresman and Company, 1986.

Knowles, M. *Using Learning Contracts.* San Francisco: Jossey-Bass, In., 1986

Kolb, D.A. *The Learning Style Inventory: Technical Manual.* Boston: McBer and Company, 1976

McBer & Co. *Kolb's Learning Style Inventory.* King of Prussia, PA, 1985.

Suelzle, M. & Borzak, L. "Stages of Fieldwork". In Borzak, L., Ed. *Field Study.* Sage Publications, 1981

Appendix A

REFLECTION
BIBLIOGRAPHY

These resources provide background on reflection, service and theories of learning.

Baskett, H.K.M. and Marsick, V.J., Eds. *Professionals' Ways of Knowing: New Findings on How to Improve Professional Education.* San Francisco: Jossey-Bass, 1992.

Belenky, M.F., Clinchy, B.M., Goldberger, N.R., and Tarule, J.M. *Women's Ways of Knowing: The Development of Self, Voice, and Mind.* New York: Basic Books, 1986.

Boud, D., Keogh, R., and Walker, D, Eds. *Reflection: Turning Experience into Learning.* New York: Routledge, 1984.

Brookfield, S.D. *Developing Critical Thinkers: Challenging Adults to Explore Alternative Ways of Thinking and Acting.* San Francisco: Jossey-Bass, 1987.

Brookfield, S.D. "Discussion." In M.W. Galbraith, Ed., *Adult Learning Methods.* Malabar, FL: Krieger, 1990.

Brookfield, S.C. *Becoming a Critically Reflective Teacher.* San Francisco: Jossey-Bass, 1995.

Clift, R.T., Houston, W.R., and Pugach, M.C., Eds, *Encouraging Reflective Practice: An Analysis of Issues and Programs.* New York: Teachers College Press, 1990.

Eyler, J. & Giles, D.E., Jr. "The Importance of Program Quality in Service-Learning" in Waterman, A., Ed. *Service-Learning Applications from the Research.* Hilldale, N.J., Earlbaum and Associates, 1997.

Eyler, J. "Comparing the Impact of Two Internship Experiences on Student Learning." *Journal of Cooperative Education,* 29(3), 41-52, 1993.

Giles, D.E., Jr. & Eyler, J. "The Theoretical Roots of Service-Learning in John Dewey: Towards a Theory of Service-Learning." *Michigan Journal of Community Service-Learning Research,*1(1), 1994.

Habermas, J. *The Theory of Communicative Action*, Vo.. 1: Reason and the Rationalization of Society. Boston: Beacon Press, 1984.

Habermas, J. The Theory of Communicative Action, Vo.. 2: *Life World and System: A Critique of Functionalist Reason.* Boston: Beacon, 1987.

Harri-Augstein, S., and Thomas, L. *Learning Conversations: The Self-Organized Learning Way to Personal and Organizational Growth.* New York: Routledge, 1991.

King, P.M., and Kitchener, K.S. *Developing Reflective Judgment: Understanding and Promoting Intellectual Growth and Critical Thinking in Adolescents and Adults.* San Francisco: Jossey-Bass, 1994.

Kolb, D.A. *Experiential Learning: Experience As the Source of Learning and Development.* New Jersey: Prentice-Hall, Inc., 1984.

Mezirow, J. and Associates. *Fostering Critical Reflection in Adulthood.* San Francisco: Jossey-Bass, 1990.

Pugach, M.C., and Johnson, L.J. "Developing Reflective Practice Through Structured Dialogue." In R.T. Clift, W.R. Houston, and M.C. Pugach, Eds., *Encouraging Reflective Practice: An Analysis of Issues and Programs.* New York: Teachers College Press, 1990.

Schon, D.A., ED. *The Reflective Practitioner: How Professionals Think in Action.* New York: Basic Books, Inc., 1983.

Schon, D.A., Ed. *Educating The Reflective Practitioner: Toward a New Design for Teaching and Learning in the Professions.* San Francisco: Jossey-Bass, 1987.

Schon, D.A., Ed. *The Reflective Turn: Case Studies in and on Educational Practice.* New York: Teachers College press, 1991.

Silcox, H.C. *A How-To Guide to Reflection: Adding Cognitive Learning to Community Service Programs.* Philadelphia: Brighton Press, Inc.,1993.

Appendix B

REFLECTION
GUIDES & HANDBOOKS

These resources are hands-on guides dealing with the details of service-learning and reflection. If you need some more "How-to's" and tips, this is where you'll find it.

Axt, Debbi, ed. *The Break Away Site Leader Survival Manual.* Break Away: the Alternative Break Connection, Nashville, TN, 1994.

Goldsmith, Suzanne. *Journal Reflection: A Resource Guide for Community Service Leaders and Educators Engaged in Service Learning.* The American Alliance for Rights & Responsibilities, Washington, D.C., 1995.

Brevard Community College Center for Service-Learning. *Reportage: Reflections on Learning.* Brevard Community College.

Florida Campus Compact. *The Tackle Box "Fishing for How-to-do-it Tools" Service-Learning Technical Assistance Publication.* Vol. 1 No. 1, April, 1995. "Reflection: Tools & Outcomes."

Willette, Zac et al. *Curriculum Based Alternative Breaks: the Manual.* Break Away: the Alternative Break Connection, Nashville, TN, 1994.

❖

Appendices

Appendix C

HELPFUL READINGS
FOR REFLECTION

These resources include actual case studies and collections of true accounts of lives affected by service. Try the reflection activity dealing with case studies (See page 70) or a journaling exercise (See page 78) in conjunction with these readings — for a good deal of food for thought.

Albert, G. *Service-Learning Reader: Reflections and Perspectives on Service.* Raleigh, N.C.: National Society for Experiential Education, 1995.

A collection of essays outlining various philosophical viewpoints on the subject of service.

Bellah, R. *Habits of the Heart: Individualism and Commitment in American Life.* Berkeley: University of California Press, 1985

This is a landmark study about the tension between individualism and the need for commitment and community life. It is very thought provoking and is regarded as a unique window to the American character.

Colby, A. *Some Do Care: Contemporary Lives of Moral Commitment.* New York: Free Press, 1992.

This is a study in moral development that interviewed people who have lived lives of commitment. The stories are fascinating and inspiring and the analysis helps to make sense of what motivates these "moral examplars" to devote their lives to helping their fellow human beings.

Coles, R. *The Call of Service: A Witness to Idealism.* Boston: Houghton Mifflin Co., 1993.

Written by the famous Harvard psychiatrist, this book is both a personal account of the meaning of service and a scholarly analysis of the types of service. Coles makes a strong case for the "call of service" as a central behavior of human social life.

Covey, S. *The Seven Habits of Highly Effective People: Restoring the Character Ethic.* New York: Simon & Schuster, 1989.

Covey tries to recapture a sense of ethical responsibility as central to effectiveness and leadership.

Daloz Parks, S.; Keen, C.H.; Keen, J.P. and Parks Daloz, L.A. *Common Fire: Lives of Commitment in a Complex World.* Boston, MA: Beacon Press, 1996.

This team of educational researchers studied more than 100 people who have dedicated their lives to the public good, revealing the kinds of experiences, relationships and opportunities that led them to seek out and sustain this kind of work.

Delve, D., Mintz, S.c., & Stewart, G.M, Eds. *Community Service as Values Education.* San Francisco: Jossey-Bass, 1990

This edited volume includes a theory of the stages of development in service-learning along with several case studies and program examples of how students learn and develop through engagement with service and reflection.

Kozol, J. *Rachel and Her Children: Homeless Family in America. New York:* Crown Publishers, 1988.

A passionate account of the plight of homeless families in the USA. The book contains personal accounts from homeless people which alternate with the author's discussion of homeless issues.

Peavey, F. *Heart Politics.* Philadelphia: New Society Publishers, 1986.

Fran Peavey's journal of her journey around the world to discover how people feel about the future in relation to today's nuclear crisis.

Rose, M. *Lives on the Boundary: The Struggles and Achievements of America's Underprepared.* New York: Free Press, 1989.

In a series of vividly written vignettes, Mike Rose describes how he has taught disadvantaged students to learn the language and codes of academic achievement. His book challenges society's prejudices about the academic abilities of the underprivileged.

Verghese, A. *My Own Country: A Doctor's Story of a Town and Its People in the Age of AIDS.* New York: Simon & Schuster, 1994.

Dr. Abraham Verghese chronicles the five years that he spent caring for AIDS patients in a rural area of eastern Tennessee.

Appendix D

REFLECTIVE
INTERVIEW GUIDE

Interview Number:_____ Date: _____

Interviewer:_____

"We are interested in your experiences with community service and your views on how this service has contributed to your understanding of social problems and issues. We are also interested in the specific kinds of learning experiences that may have influenced your understanding. We hope to be able to share the insights of students about service-learning with people who are planning programs, so we want to explore your learning process in some detail."

1. PERSONAL SERVICE HISTORY

"First, I'd like to ask you about your personal history of service. I see that your first service experience was _____. Tell me more about this." [Warm up.]

"How did you first get involved? Why did you do this?"

[Refer to subsequent experiences; ask about others. If they differ, ask:]

"I notice that you have worked with different issues/types of projects. Can you tell me how you got involved with these projects?"

"How would you describe this change in your involvement?"

"Were there specific events or moments when you realized you wanted to do something different?" [Probes:] *"Describe the moment. Was anyone else involved in this process? Who? What has kept you doing service?"*

If all experiences are similar in focus or issue, ask:

"I notice you seem to have been involved with _____ [issue/problem] for some time. Can you tell me what keeps you involved with this issue?"

2. THINKING ABOUT SOCIAL ISSUES AND PROBLEMS

"Now I'd like to ask you about your thinking about community and social issues."

"Has your thinking about social issues or the people you work with in the community changed over time?" [Probe:] *"Which? Both?"*

"Can you think of times when you were surprised by something in your service? That is, when you suddenly looked at a situation or an issue in a way that you hadn't before?

When you realized that you needed the answers to some new questions?"

[For each incident, ask:]

"Please describe the incident. What made this situation different? A puzzle? What made you want to find our more about the situation? How did it influence your thinking? What helped you reflect on this issue? [Probe:] Were there structured discussions, projects or assignments that helped you think about the issues?"

3. REFLECTIVE PROGRAM EXPERIENCE

"Now I'd like to find out more about some of the experiences you've had in differentt service programs."

[Refer to any mentioned as critical incidents in #2 above and on the service history sheet.] *"Of these experiences you've had, were there programs or classes where you had the opportunity for formal reflection?"*

[If *YES*, use Probes in column A. If *NO*, use the probes in Column B.]

Column A	*Column B*
Journals? How structured?	Just talking with others? Who?
Written Assignments?	Personal journals?
Discussions?	Discussions?
Making Presentations?	Group Activities?
Projects?	Reading?
Reading?	Listening to others?
Training/Orientation?	Training/Orientation?
Lectures? Other?	Other?

"Were there other reflection experiences? Please describe."

4. REFLECTIONS ON REFLECTION

[Ask for both informal and formal as reported in 3a/3b above. If NO reflective experiences are reported, go to #5.]

"Now I'd like to find out if/how these experiences affected your thinking. Did they help you to understand issues more fully?"

"Can you think of an example of an assigment in a service-learning class or program that helped you understand the issues you were working with more clearly?"

[Probes for each example:]

"Did it help you understand something as more than just theory?"

"Did it help you apply some of the things you were learning in the classroom to community issues?"

"Were there any assignments or activities that left you with new questions?"

[Be alert to redundancy from incidents mentioned in #2. Probe further from examples given in #2.]

"Of all the experiences that shifted your way of understanding community issues and service, which was the most valuable for you? Why?"

"From your experience, what would you say is the most effective type of reflection? Why?"

5. SUMMARY OF LEARNING

"What have you learned from community service that you might not have learned in the classroom alone?"

"Is there anything else we should know to help us understand the impact of service-learning on its participants?"

"Thank you."

SOURCE
Janet Eyler & Dwight Giles,
Vanderbilt University

Appendices